A TEXT BOOK OF

PHARMACOGNOSY-IV

THIRD YEAR B. PHARM – SEMESTER V
(FOR GTU & UPTU)

S. B. GOKHALE

M. Pharm., A. I. C.

Former-Co-ordinator
RC Patel College of Pharma Education & Research
Shirpur - 425405 (M.S.)

Dr. C. K. KOKATE

M. Pharm., Ph. D., F.G.A.E.S. (Germany)

President,
Indian Society of Pharmacognosy
and
Vice-chancellor,
KLE University,
JNMC Campus, Nehru Nagar,
Belgaum - 590010 (Karnataka)

A. P. PUROHIT

M. Pharm., A. I. C.

Asst. Professor and Head,
Department of Pharmacognosy,
B. V.'s Poona College of Pharmacy and Research Centre,
Pune - 411 038 (M.S.)

NIRALI PRAKASHAN

N0884

PHARMACOGNOSY-IV (GTU)

ISBN 978-93-83073-17-7

First Edition : **May 2013**

© : **Authors**

Published By :
NIRALI PRAKASHAN
Abhyudaya Pragati, 1312, Shivaji Nagar,
Off J.M. Road, Behind Medinova Centre,
PUNE – 411005
Tel - (020) 25512336/37/39, Fax - (020) 25511379
Email : niralipune@pragationline.com

Printed at
Repro Knowledgecast Limited
India

DISTRIBUTION CENTRES

PUNE
Nirali Prakashan
119, Budhwar Peth, Jogeshwari Mandir Lane
Pune 411002, Maharashtra
Tel : (020) 2445 2044, 66022708 Fax : (020) 2445 1538
Email : bookorder@pragationline.com

MUMBAI
Nirali Prakashan
385, S.V.P. Road, Rasdhara Co-op. Hsg. Society Ltd.,
Girgaum, Mumbai 400004, Maharashtra
Tel : (022) 2385 6339 / 2386 9976, Fax : (022) 2386 9976
Email : niralimumbai@pragationline.com

DISTRIBUTION BRANCHES

NAGPUR
Pratibha Book Distributors
Above Maratha Mandir, Shop No. 3, First Floor,
Rani Jhanshi Square, Sitabuldi, Nagpur 440012,
Maharashtra, Tel : (0712) 254 7129, Mob : 98222 01952

NASIK
Nirali Prakashan
741, Gaydhani Sankul, First Floor, Raviwar Karanja,
Nasik 422001, Maharashtra
Tel : (0253) 250 6438, Mob : 94222 53538

HYDERABAD
Nirali Book House
22, Shyam Enclave, 4-5-947, Badi Chowdi
Hyderabad 500095, Andhra Pradesh
Tel : (040) 6554 5313, Mob : 94400 30608
Email: niralibooks@yahoo.com

JALGAON
Nirali Prakashan
34, V. V. Golani Market, Navi Peth, Jalgaon 425001,
Maharashtra, Tel : (0257) 222 0395
Mob : 94234 91860

KOLHAPUR
Nirali Prakashan
New Mahadvar Road,
Kedar Plaza, 1st Floor Opp. IDBI Bank,
Kolhapur 416 012, Maharashtra. Mob : 9850046155

BENGALURU
Pragati Book House
House No. 1,Sanjeevappa Lane, Avenue Road Cross,
Opp. Rice Church, Bangalore – 560002.
Tel : (080) 64513344, 64513355,
Mob : 9880582331, 9845021552
Email:bharatsavla@yahoo.com

CHENNAI
Pragati Books
9/1, Montieth Road, Behind Taas Mahal, Egmore, Chennai 600008 Tamil Nadu
Tel : (044) 6518 3535, Mob : 94440 01782 / 98450 21552 / 98805 82331
Email : bharatsavla@yahoo.com

RETAIL OUTLETS

PUNE

Pragati Book Centre
157, Budhwar Peth, Opp. Ratan Talkies,
Pune 411002, Maharashtra
Tel : (020) 2445 8887 / 6602 2707, Fax : (020) 2445 8887

Pragati Book Centre
Amber Chamber, 28/A, Budhwar Peth,
Appa Balwant Chowk, Pune : 411002, Maharashtra,
Tel : (020) 20240335 / 66281669
Email : pbcpune@pragationline.com

Pragati Book Centre
676/B, Budhwar Peth, Opp. Jogeshwari Mandir,
Pune 411002, Maharashtra
Tel : (020) 6601 7784 / 6602 0855
Email : pbcpune@pragationline.com

PBC Book Sellers & Stationers
152, Budhwar Peth, Pune 411002, Maharashtra
Tel : (020) 2445 2254 / 6609 2463

MUMBAI

Pragati Book Corner
Indira Niwas, 111 - A, Bhavani Shankar Road, Dadar (W), Mumbai 400028, Maharashtra
Tel : (022) 2422 3526 / 6662 5254
Email : pbcmumbai@pragationline.com

PREFACE

Gujarat Technological University Ahemadabad, has revised the syllabus of Bachelor of Pharmacy from 2009-10, with introduction of semester system. The subjects and their contents have been updated, taking into consideration the developments in pharmacy profession.

Phytochemical evaluation, modern analytical techniques for screening of herbal drugs, herbal cosmetics, and market products are the new chapters added to the subject Pharmacognosy.

Brief account of plant based industries and information of institutions involved in work of medicinal and aromatic plants in India are the special features that have been incorporated.

We are pleased to introduce **Pharmacognosy-IV** by offering every justice to all the features of syllabi and hope the students shall be benefited by our efforts.

We are thankful to publisher Shri Dineshbhai Furia, Shri Jigneshbhai Furai and Staff members of Nirali Prakashan for their co-operation in brining out this book.

May 2013

S. B. GOKHALE
C. K. KOKATE
A. P. PUROHIT

SYLLABUS

Pharmacognosy – IV

Third Year B. Pharm : Semester – V

1. Biosynthetic studies & Basic metabolic pathways. Brief introduction to biogenesis of secondary Metabolites of Pharmaceutical importance.

2. Alkaloids:

   Sources, cultivation, collection, processing, commercial varieties, chemical constituents, substituents, adulterants, uses, diagnostic macroscopic and microscopic features and specific chemical tests of following alkaloid containing drugs:

   i. Pyridine – Piperidine:

   Tobacco, Areca, Lobelia, Hemlock

   ii. Tropane:

   Datura, Belladonna, Hyocyamus, Withania, Dubosia, Coca

   iii. Quinoline and Isoquinoline:

   Cinhona, Ipecac, Opium, Camptotheca

   iv. Indole:

   Ergot, Rauwolfia, Catharanthus, Nux vomica, Physostigma

   v. Imidazole:

   Pilocarpus

   vi. Steroidal:

   Veratrum, Kurchi

   vii. Alkaloidal Amine:

   Ephedra, Colchicum

   viii. Purines:

   Coffee, Tea, Cola

   ix. Quinazoline:

   Vasaka

   x. Diterpene Alkaloids:

   Aconite

3. Concept of stereoisomerism taking examples of natural products.

❖ ❖ ❖

CONTENTS

❖ ❖ ❖

Chapter 1

BIOSYNTHESIS AND BIOGENESIS OF SECONDARY METABOLITES

AN INTRODUCTION TO BIOGENESIS OF PHYTOPHARMACEUTICALS

The living plant may be considered as a biosynthetic laboratory not only for the primary metabolites like sugars, amino acids and fatty acids that are utilized as food by man, but also for a multitude of secondary products of pharmaceutical significance such as glycosides, alkaloids, flavonoids, volatile oils, etc. A higher plant is a solar-powered biochemical factory which manufactures both primary and secondary metabolites from air, water, minerals and sunlight. Primary metabolites are substances that are widely distributed in nature, occurring in one form or another in virtually all organisms and are needed for general growth and physiological development, because of their basic cell metabolism. Secondary metabolites are biosynthetically derived from primary metabolites but are more limited in distribution, usually being restricted to a taxonomic group. They may represent chemical adaptations to environmental stresses, or they may serve as defensive, protective or offensive chemicals against microorganisms, insects and higher herbivorous predators. They are sometimes considered to be waste or secretory products of plant metabolism. In terms of cellular economy, secondary products are in general expensive to produce and accumulate, and are, therefore frequently present in plants in much smaller quantities than are primary metabolites.

The photosynthetic process in green plants is essential for all animal life on earth, since it initiates conversion of solar energy into organic carbon compounds which in turn are used to produce essential foods. The photosynthetic sequence in green plants is capture of light and use of its energy to liberate molecular oxygen from water to synthesize organic compounds from carbon dioxide, nitrate and sulphate. The major source of carbon is usually glucose, which is photosynthesized in green plants. The recent advances in the field of biochemistry have greatly clarified enzyme-catalyzed and interrelated reactions resulting in formation of primary metabolites and their role in the synthesis of secondary products, many of which are used by man. Since these secondary products do not occur in all plants, their biochemistry was ignored until several decades by those interested in chemical plant physiology. Nevertheless, many of them are extremely important as pharmaceutical agents.

The various biosynthetic reactions occurring in plant cells are enzyme-dependent, wherein enzymes act as catalysts of metabolism and it is through the control of enzymatic activity that plant metabolism is directed into specific biosynthetic pathways. The enzymatic reactions are reversible and in plants, many a time, the secondary metabolites are synthesized and hydrolyzed under the influence of more or less specific enzymes.

The elucidation of biosynthetic pathways in plants for the production of various plant metabolites has been extensively examined by means of isotopically labelled precursors. With the advancement of tracer technology, it is possible to incorporate isotopes into presumed precursors of plant metabolites and use as markers in biogenetic experiments. With the use of radioactive carbon (^{14}C) and hydrogen (^{3}H) and to a lesser extent sulphur (^{36}S) and phosphorous (^{32}P), it is possible to understand various biosynthetic pathways. A labelled nitrogen atom may give more specific information about the biosynthesis of alkaloids, proteins and amino acids.

The most notable success by use of isotopically labelled precursors was achieved by Birch in the biosynthetic investigations of mould metabolites such as 6-methylsalicylic acid and griseofulvin from ^{14}C-labelled acetate.

The basic carbon reduction cycle by which carbon dioxide is converted to sugar phosphates is of primary importance, both as an energy yielding process and also as a source of various metabolic intermediates. Two biosynthetic pathways of special importance in breakdown of sugar are pentose phosphate cycle (direct pathway) and glycolysis. The hexose phosphate is oxidized first into carbon-dioxide and pentose phosphate in direct pathway.

The pentose phosphate formed due to biosynthetic degradation may then be utilized as such or otherwise converted by a series of metabolic reactions into triose phosphate or by a reversal of glycolysis, into a hexose; however, in glycolysis, hexose phosphate is split hydrolytically to yield triose phosphate, which can then be oxidized. Although the total number of natural products for which biosynthetic investigations have been carried out are quite limited compared with the diversity and number of natural products, our accumulation of knowledge in biogenetic field makes it possible to predict the gross biogenetic origin of practically all plant products.

Table 1.1: The primary and secondary metabolites derived from carbon metabolism in plants

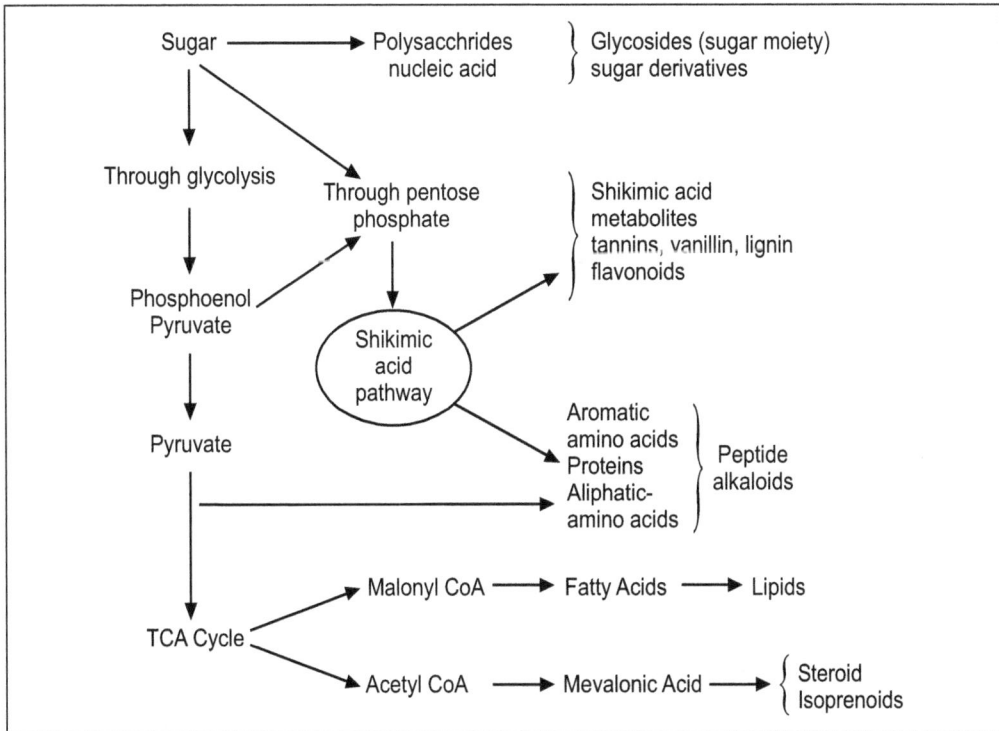

Sugar ⟶ Polysacchrides nucleic acid } Glycosides (sugar moiety) sugar derivatives

Through glycolysis

Through pentose phosphate } Shikimic acid metabolites tannins, vanillin, lignin flavonoids

Phosphoenol Pyruvate

Shikimic acid pathway

Pyruvate

Aromatic amino acids Proteins Aliphatic- amino acids } Peptide alkaloids

Malonyl CoA ⟶ Fatty Acids ⟶ Lipids

TCA Cycle

Acetyl CoA ⟶ Mevalonic Acid ⟶ { Steroid Isoprenoids

SHIKIMIC ACID PATHWAY

The Shikimic acid is a key intermediate from carbohydrate for the biosynthesis of $C_6 - C_3$ units (phenylpropane derivatives). Besides serving as precursor for the biosynthesis of amino acids, Shikimic acid is also an intermediate in production of tannins, flavones, coumarins and vanillin.

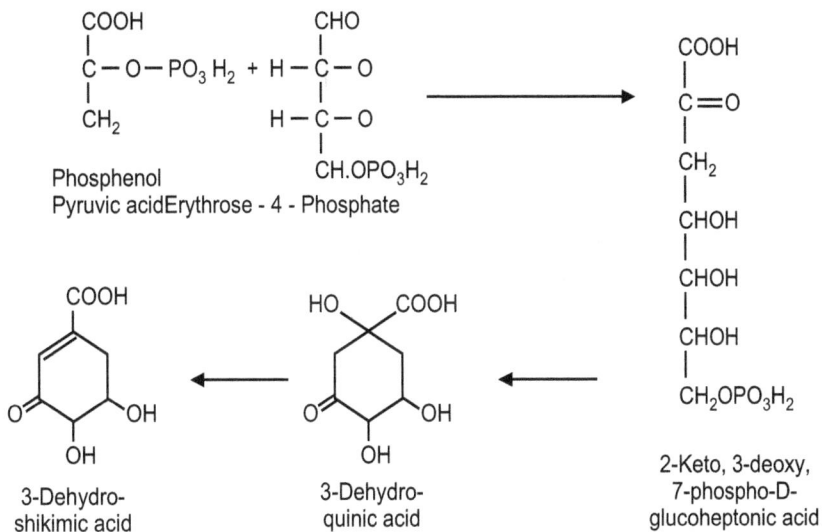

$$
\begin{array}{l}
\text{COOH} \\
| \\
\text{C}-\text{O}-\text{PO}_3\text{H}_2 \\
| \\
\text{CH}_2
\end{array}
+
\begin{array}{l}
\text{CHO} \\
| \\
\text{H}-\text{C}-\text{O} \\
| \\
\text{H}-\text{C}-\text{O} \\
| \\
\text{CH.OPO}_3\text{H}_2
\end{array}
\longrightarrow
\begin{array}{l}
\text{COOH} \\
| \\
\text{C}=\text{O} \\
| \\
\text{CH}_2 \\
| \\
\text{CHOH} \\
| \\
\text{CHOH} \\
| \\
\text{CHOH} \\
| \\
\text{CH}_2\text{OPO}_3\text{H}_2
\end{array}
$$

Phosphenol Pyruvic acid Erythrose - 4 - Phosphate

2-Keto, 3-deoxy, 7-phospho-D-glucoheptonic acid

3-Dehydro-shikimic acid ← 3-Dehydro-quinic acid ←

3-Dehydro-
shikimic acid

3-Dehydro-
quinic acid

COOH

HO OH

OH

Shikimic acid

COOH

CH₂

O CH COOH

OH

Chorismic acid

COOH

NH₂

Anthranilic acid

C — CH₂ — CH — COOH

N H NH₂

H

Tryptophan

COOH

CO

HOOC CH₂

H OH

Prephenic acid

COOH

C = O

CH₂

Phenyl pyruvic acid

COOH

CH — NH₂

CH₂

Phenylalanine

COOH

C = O

CH₂

OH

p-Hydroxy phenyl pyruvic acid

COOH

CH — NH₂

CH₂

OH

Tyrosine

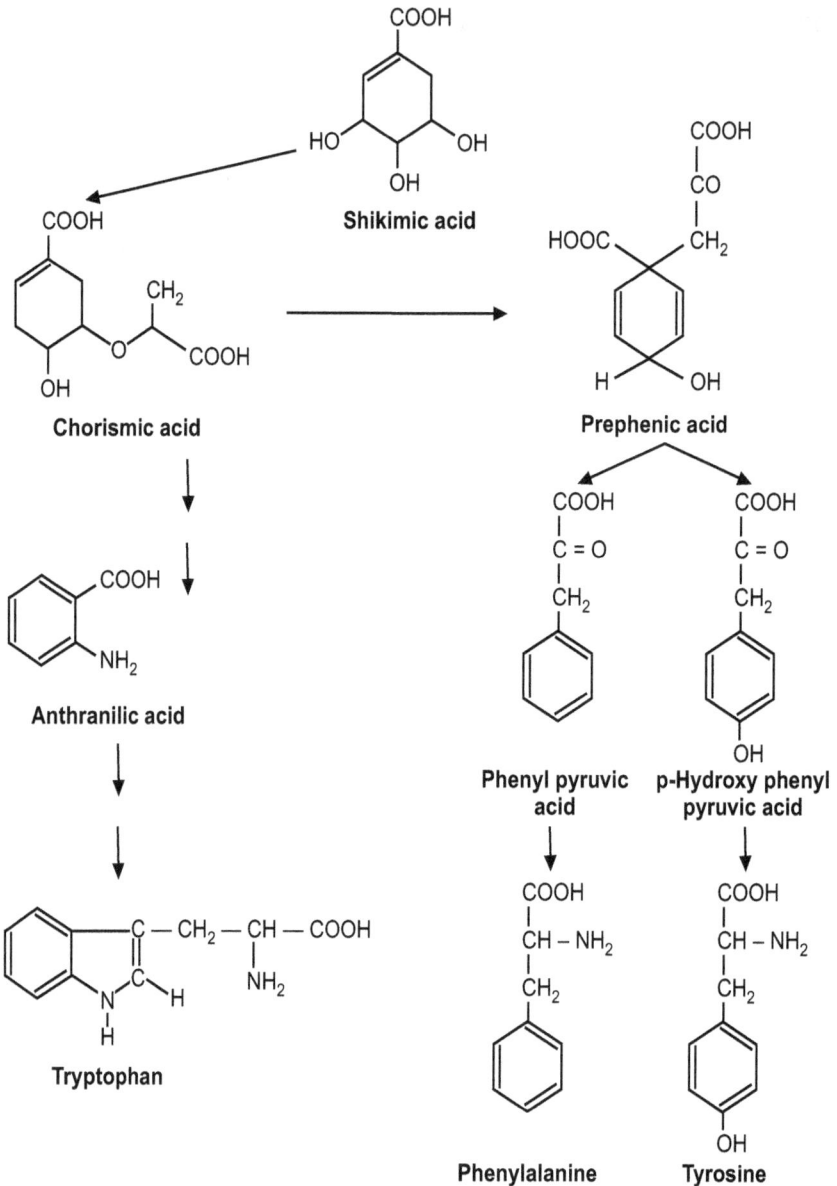

Production of Amino Acids by Shikimic Acid Pathway

BIOSYNTHESIS OF GLYCOSIDES

The metabolic process of glycoside formation essentially consists of two parts: The first part of biosynthesis is the reactions by means of which various type of aglycones are formed, where as the other part of biosynthesis process takes into account metabolic pathway involving coupling of aglycones with sugar moiety. The synthesis of glycosides in plant cells involves interaction of nucleotide glycoside such as UDP-glucose with alcoholic or phenolic group of second compound aglycones. Such glycosides, called as o-glycosides, are commonly found in plant. The other glycosides also occur in nature in which the linkage is through carbon (C-glycosides), nitrogen (N-glycosides) or sulphur (S- glycosides).

The principal pathway of glycoside formation involves the transfer of uridylyl group from uridine triphosphate (UTP) to sugar-1-phosphate and the enzymes catalyzing this reaction are known as uridylyl transferases. The subsequent reaction controlled by enzymatic system glycosyl transferases involves transfer of sugar from uridine diphosphate to aglycone moiety resulting in formation of glycoside.

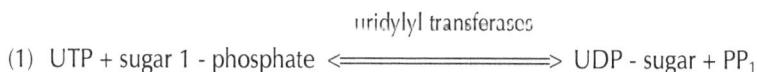

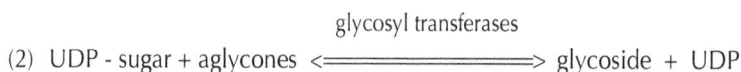

$$\text{uridylyl transferases}$$

(1) UTP + sugar 1 - phosphate $\Longleftrightarrow$ UDP - sugar + PP$_1$

$$\text{glycosyl transferases}$$

(2) UDP - sugar + aglycones $\Longleftrightarrow$ glycoside + UDP

The sugars present in glycosides may be monosaccharides such as rhamnose, glucose and fucose or deoxysugars such as digitoxose or cymarose as in cardiac glycosides.

The aglycones of cardio-active glycosides are steroidal in nature. They are the derivatives of cyclopentenophenanthrene ring containing an unsaturated lactone ring attached to C_{17}, a $14 - alpha$ hydroxyl group and a cisjuncture of rings C and D. The knowledge of steroidal biosynthesis is derived from studies of cholesterol production through acetate → mevalonate → isopentenyl pyrophosphate → squalene pathway. The biosynthesis of cholesterol involves cyclization of aliphatic triterpene-squalene.

In plants, sapogenins occur in the form of their glycosides, i.e. saponins. The neutral saponins are derivatives of steroids with side chains whereas acid saponins possess triterpenoid structures. The main pathway for biogenesis of both types of sapogenins is similar. However, a branch occurs, probably after formation of triterpenoid hydrocarbon-squalene which leads to cyclic triterpenoids in one direction and spirochaetal steroids in other direction. The bioproduction of squalene, cholesterol and various steroidal compounds including the aglycones is outlined.

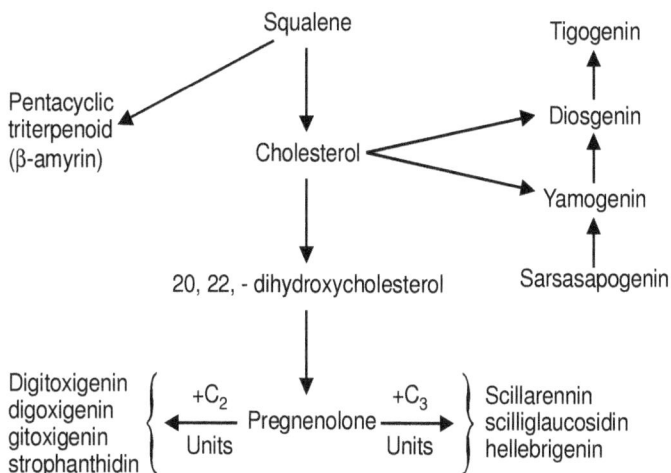

Some secondary products of cholesterol metabolism

The knowledge of biosynthesis of anthracene aglycones has been obtained from studies with micro-organisms, especially *Penicillium islanidicum*. An intermediate polyketomethylene acid is probably produced from 8 acetate units which on intramolecular condensation forms anthraquinone.

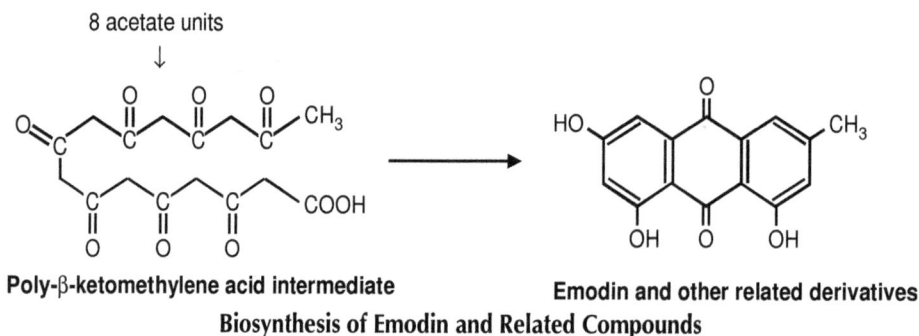

8 acetate units

↓

Poly-β-ketomethylene acid intermediate　　　　　**Emodin and other related derivatives**

Biosynthesis of Emodin and Related Compounds

A second metabolic pathway for production of anthraquinone is through Shikimic acid as operative in some plants of Rubiaceae. The biosynthesis of alizarin reveals that ring A is derived from Shikimic acid, while mevalonic acid is incorporated into ring C.

Shikimic acid ⟶ [A] [C] ⟵ Mevalonic acid

Alizarin

Biosynthesis of Alizarin from *Rubia tinctorum* (Rubiaceae)

The aglycones of pharmaceutically significant cyanogenetic glycosides are phenylpropanoid compounds derived from amino acids phenylalanine and tyrosine which are the products of Shikimic acid pathway. The aglycones of linamarin are derived from valine and that of lotaustralin from isoleucine.

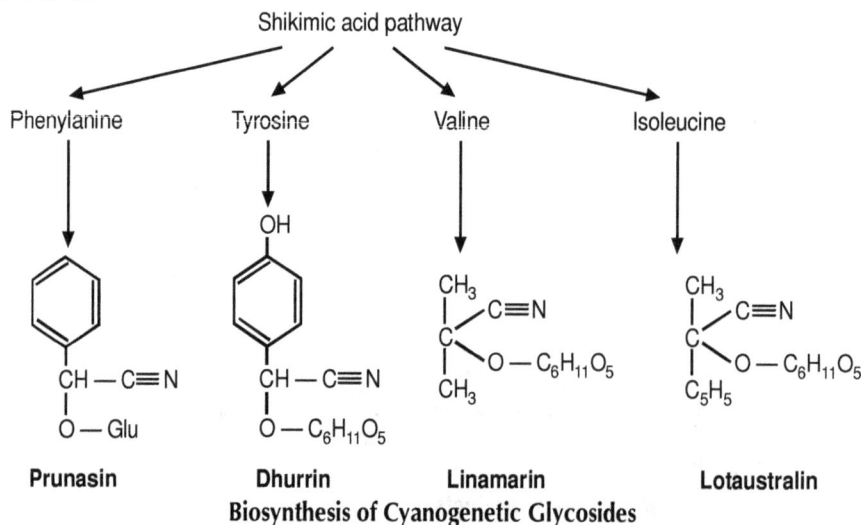

Shikimic acid pathway

Phenylanine　　　Tyrosine　　　Valine　　　Isoleucine

Prunasin　　　**Dhurrin**　　　**Linamarin**　　　**Lotaustralin**

Biosynthesis of Cyanogenetic Glycosides

The aglycones of isothiocynate glycosides may consist of either aliphatic derivative biosynthesized via acetate pathway or aromatic derivatives produced biosynthetically via Shikimic acid route.

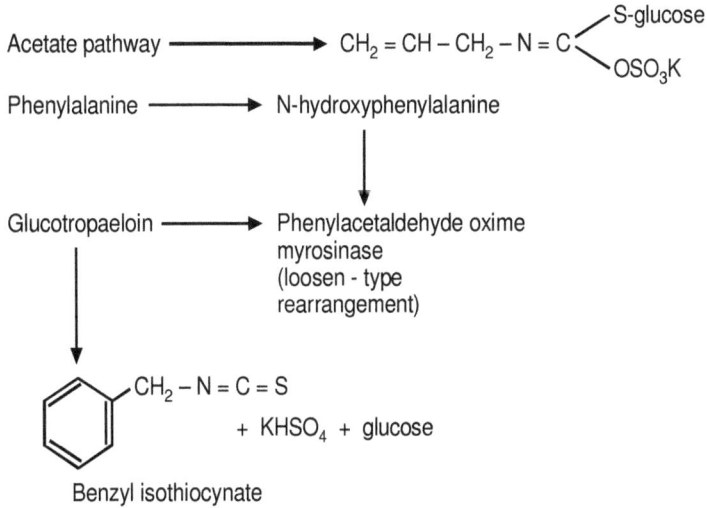

Acetate pathway ⟶ $CH_2 = CH - CH_2 - N = C \begin{smallmatrix} \diagup S\text{-glucose} \\ \diagdown OSO_3K \end{smallmatrix}$

Phenylalanine ⟶ N-hydroxyphenylalanine

Glucotropaeloin ⟶ Phenylacetaldehyde oxime
myrosinase
(loosen - type
rearrangement)

$CH_2 - N = C = S$
+ $KHSO_4$ + glucose

Benzyl isothiocynate

Biosynthesis of Isothiocynate Aglycone

The aglycones of flavones glycoside are derived from both acetate metabolism and Shikimic acid pathway. The A ring arises by head-to-tail condensation of two malonyl Co-A units and acetyl Co–A. The B ring and C_3 unit come from a C_6 - C_3 precursor, which may be cinnamic acid itself.

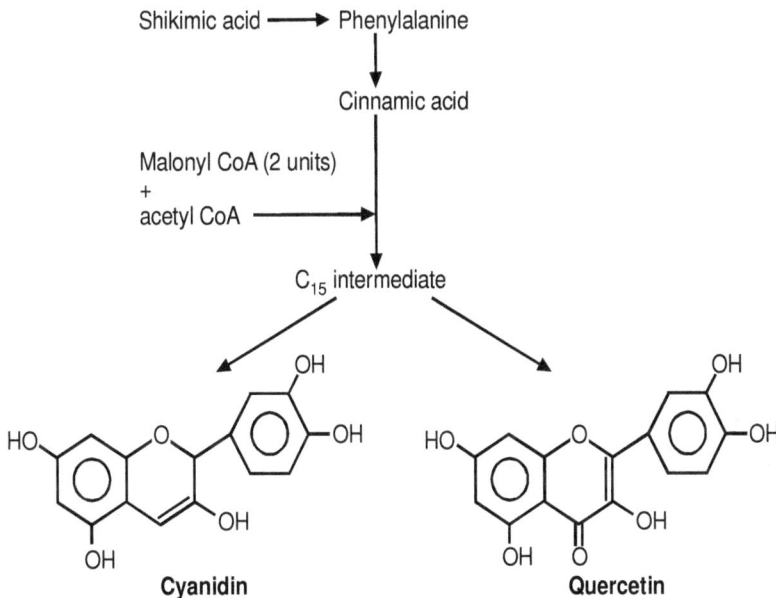

Shikimic acid ⟶ Phenylalanine

Cinnamic acid

Malonyl CoA (2 units)
+
acetyl CoA ⟶

C_{15} intermediate

Cyanidin

Quercetin

Biosynthetic pathways to Flavonoid Aglycones

The aromatic nuclei of alcohol, aldehyde, lactone and phenol glycosides are derived from C_6 - C_3 precursors formed via Shikimic acid pathway.

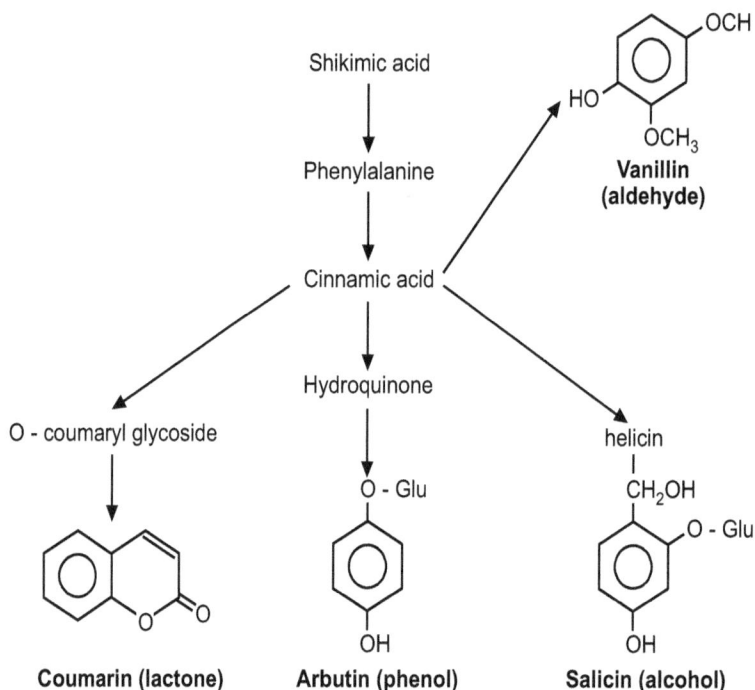

Biosynthesis of Lactone, Phenol, Alcohol and Aldehyde Glycosides

BIOSYNTHESIS OF ALKALOIDS

The biosynthesis of different groups of alkaloids has now been investigated to some extent using precursors labelled with radioactive atoms. Some work has, however, been published in the area of enzymology of alkaloid biosynthesis, some exceptions being in studies of *ergot* and *Amaryllidaceae* alkaloids. The biosynthetic pathways for pharmacognostically important alkaloids are given below.

1. Alkaloids derived from ornithine

The studies have revealed that ornithine is incorporated into both pyrrolidine and tropane alkaloids. Ornithine is incorporated stereospecifically and asymmetrically into pyrollidine ring of tropane nucleus, the alpha-carbon of ornithine becoming the C 1 of tropine nucleus. The remaining three carbon atoms are derived from acetate, thus completing piperidine moiety. Methionine serves as the methyl group donor whereas phenylalanine is the precursor of tropic acid. The different alkaloids derived from ornithine are grouped together.

Hygrine

Ornithine

COOH

Δ^1-pyrroline

Nicotinic acid

Nicotine

Ornithine

Methionine

N CH$_3$

CH$_2$
|
CHOH
|
CH$_2$

2 Acetate units

Tropine

Acetate

Methionine

N CH$_3$

CH — COOCH$_3$
|
CH — OCO — C$_6$H$_5$
|
CH$_2$

Phenylalanine

CH — COOH
|
CH$_2$OH

Tropic acid

Cocaine

N CH$_3$ CHOCO — CH — C$_6$H$_5$
|
CH$_2$OH

Hyoscyamine / atropine

N CH$_3$ CHOCO — CH — C$_6$H$_5$
|
CH$_2$OH

Scopolamine

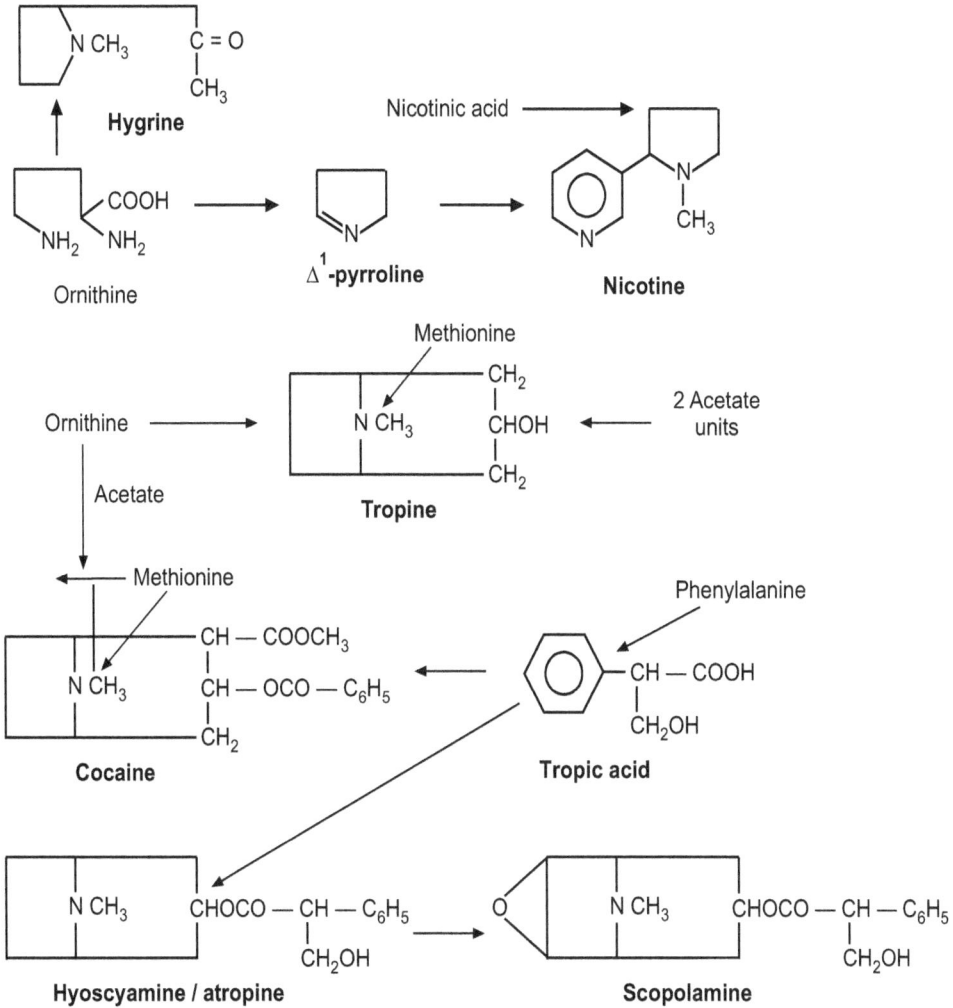

Some Alkaloids, Derived From Ornithine

2. Alkaloids derived from Lysine

Lysine and its associated compounds are responsible for the biogenesis of anabasine, lupinine, isopelletierine and other related alkaloids -

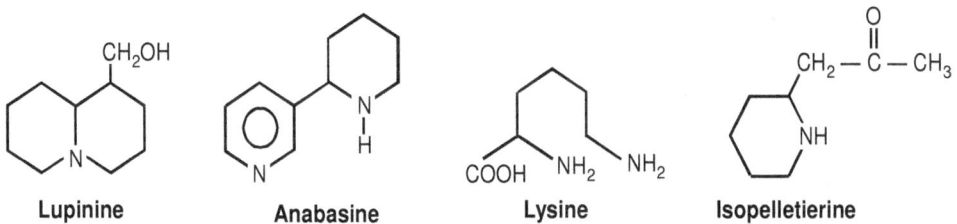

CH$_2$OH

Lupinine

Anabasine

COOH   NH$_2$ NH$_2$

Lysine

CH$_2$ — C — CH$_3$ (with C=O)

Isopelletierine

Some Alkaloids derived from Lysine

Ornithine

→ Methylation →

8 - N - methylomithine

Phenylalanine

Decarboxylation

4-methyl amino butanal

← Oxidation ←

N-methylputrescine

Phenyl pyravic acid

N methyl - Δ - pyrrolinium salt

→ Acetoacetic acid →

Hygine

Tropic acid
+
Tropine

Dehydrogenation

Tropinone

← Aldol Condensation ←

l-Hyoscyamine

Reduction

Tropine

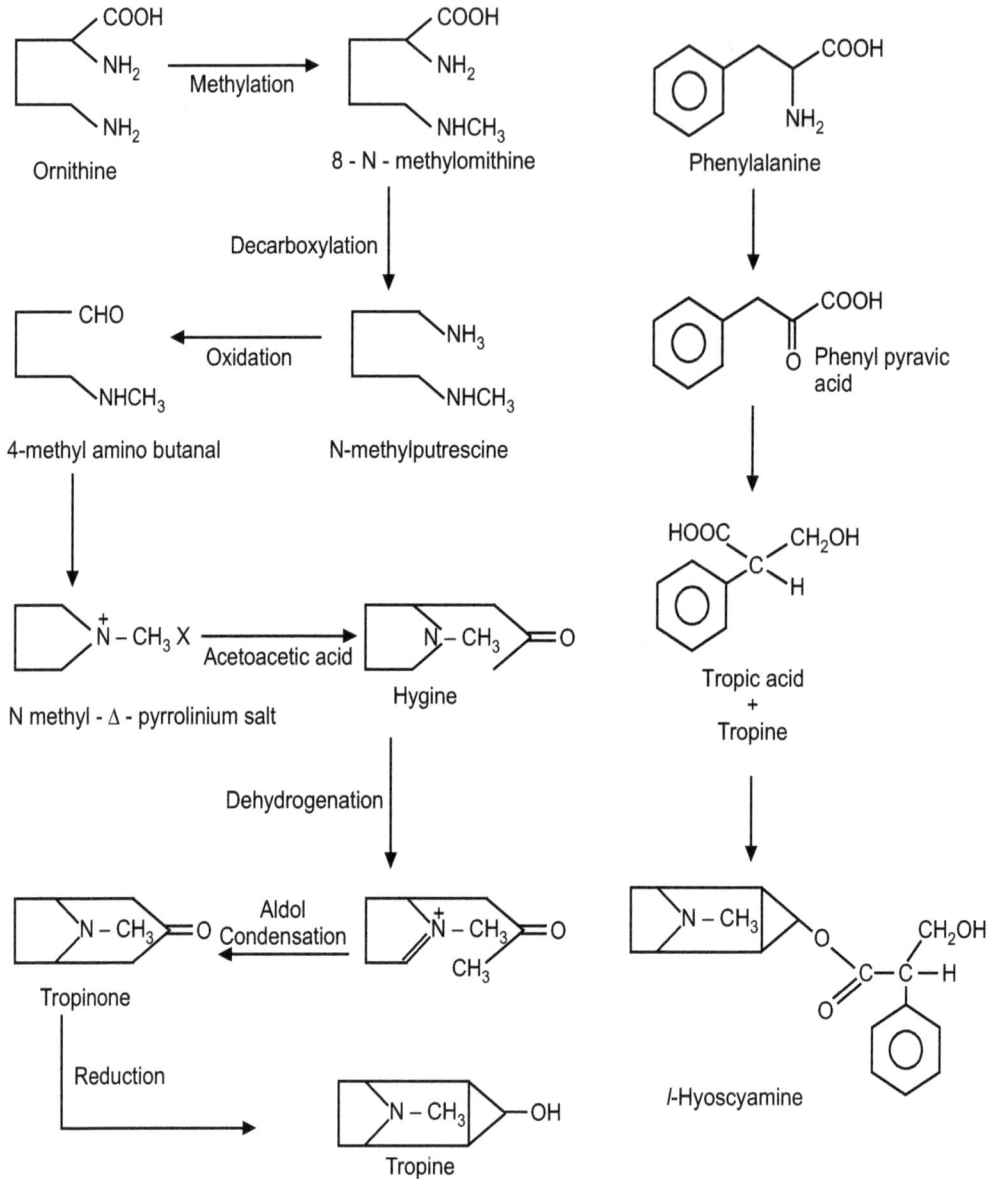

Biosynthesis of l-Hyoscyamine

3.　Alkaloids derived from Phenylalanine, Tyrosine and related Amino acids

These amino acids and their corresponding decarboxylation products serve as the precursors for a large number of alkaloids including ephedrine, colchicine and opium alkaloids. Earlier it was shown that tyrosine and dopamine could serve as precursors of morphine. It was also proved that the first of the opium alkaloids synthesized is thebaine, followed by codeine and morphine.

Phenylalanine → Ephedrine

Phenylalanine → Mescaline

Tyrosine → Papavorine

Thebaine → Codeine → Morphine

Tyrosine → Dihydroxyphenylalanine (and dopamine)

Dihydroxyphenylalanine (and dopamine) → Emetine

Dihydroxyphenylalanine (and dopamine) → Colchicine

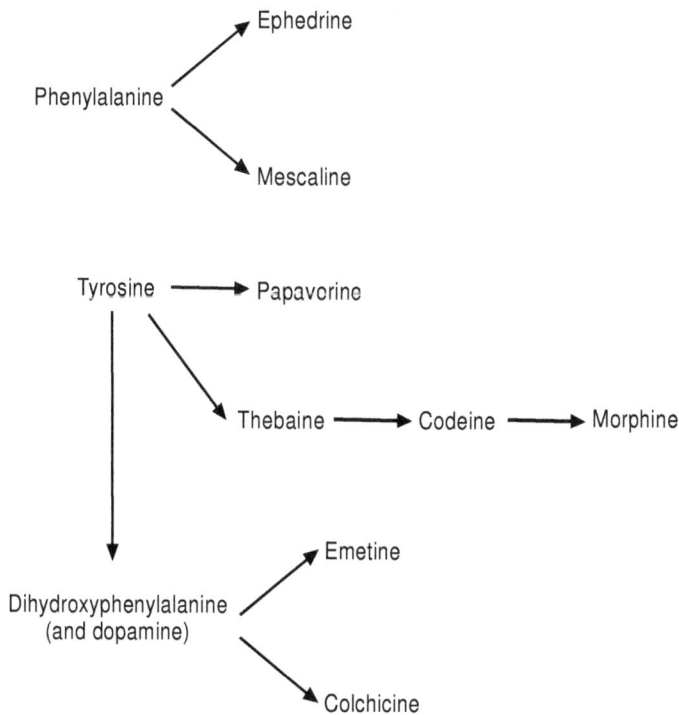

Some alkaloids derived from phenylalanine, tyrosine and their derivatives

4. Alkaloids derived from tryptophan

The biosynthesis of quinine and related alkaloids of cinchona proceeds through a route indicating transformation of indole to quinoline. With regard with the source of non-tryptamine derived portion, however, participation of a monoterpene glucoside, secologanin, from mevalonate-pathway has been demonstrated. The most significant feature of quinine biosynthesis is cleavage of benzypyrrole ring of tryptophan moiety and rearrangement to form the quinoline nucleus.

Tryptophan and its decarboxylation product tryptamine, serve as the precursors for biosynthesis of a large class of indole alkaloids. The non-tryptophan portions of alkaloids are, however, derived from monoterpenoid precursors which are designated as the *Coryanthe, Iboga* and *Aspidosperma* types. The reactive form of terpene involves an aldehyde group. The loss of one carbon atom during biogenesis to give C_9 unit appears to be largely common. It is believed that *Coryanthe* type monoterpenoid moiety is metabolically most primitive. Condensation of tryptamine (or tryptophan) with secologanin, a monoterpene glucoside, gives rise to a nitrogenous glucoside, vincoside, from which a great variety of indole alkaloids, including monomeric alkaloids in *Catharanthus roseus,* are formed. The Rauwolfia alkaloids such as reserpine, rescinnamine, serpentine, ajmaline, etc. are derived from a *Coryanthe* type monoterpenoid precursor.

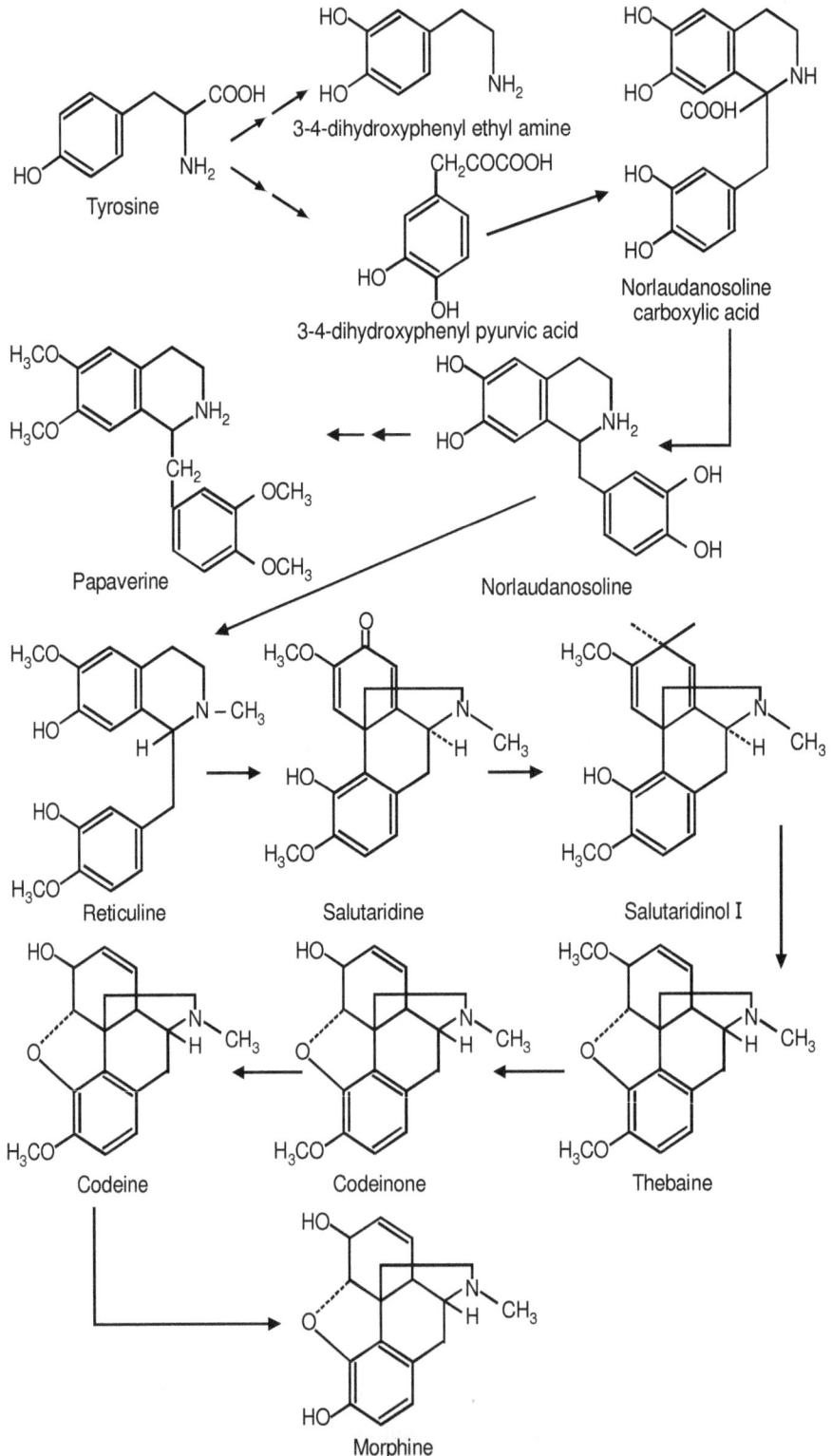

Biosynthetic Pattern of Narcotine, Thebaine, Codeine and Morphine

The ergot alkaloids are also derived from a combination of acetate metabolism and tryptophan. The condensation of dimethylallyl pyrophosphate at 4-position of tryptophan takes place as the first step in pathway. Subsequently, the cyclization reactions involve production of chanoclavine 1 and agroclavine. The latter undergoes stepwise oxidation to elymoclavine and eventually lysergic acid. The carboxyl group of lysergic acid forms a peptide linkage with an amino group of a variety of amino acids to yield the medicinally important ergot alkaloids.

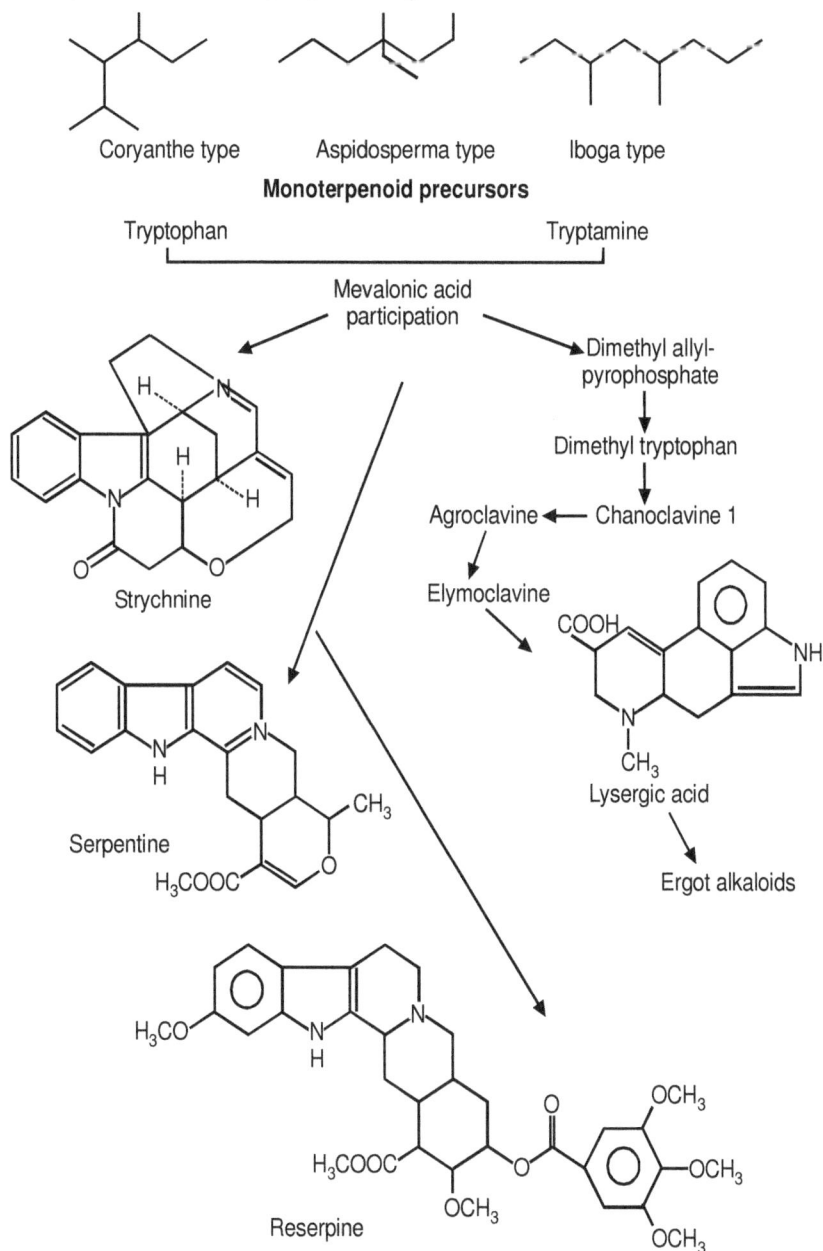

Coryanthe type   Aspidosperma type   Iboga type

Monoterpenoid precursors

Tryptophan   Tryptamine

Mevalonic acid participation

→ Dimethyl allyl-pyrophosphate

Dimethyl tryptophan

Agroclavine ← Chanoclavine 1

Strychnine

Elymoclavine

Lysergic acid

Serpentine

Ergot alkaloids

Reserpine

Biosynthesis of Some Indole Alkaloids

Coryantheal ⟶

Vincoside

Quinine

Tryptophan

Secologanin

Tryptamine

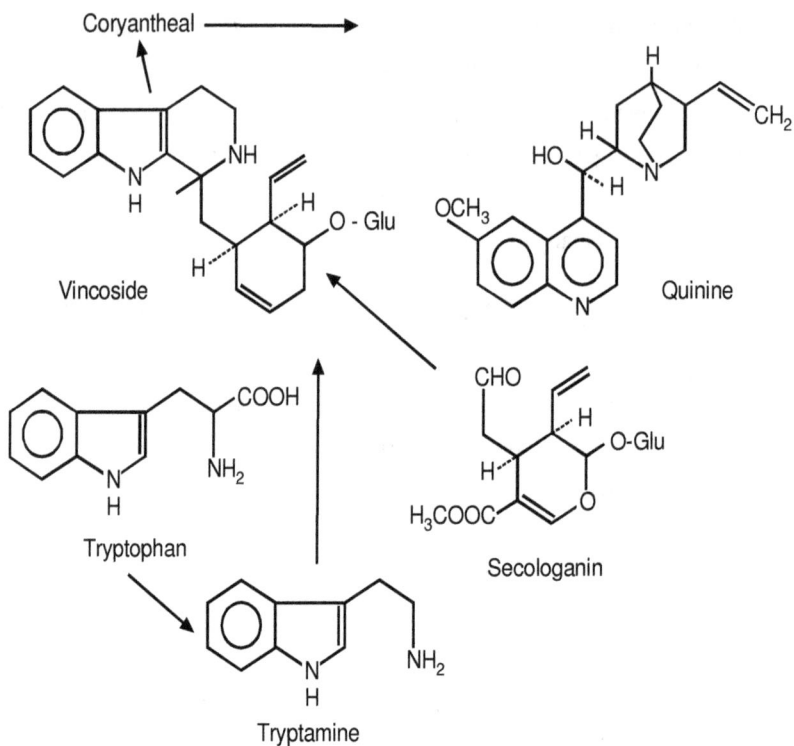

Biosynthesis of Some Quinoline Alkaloids

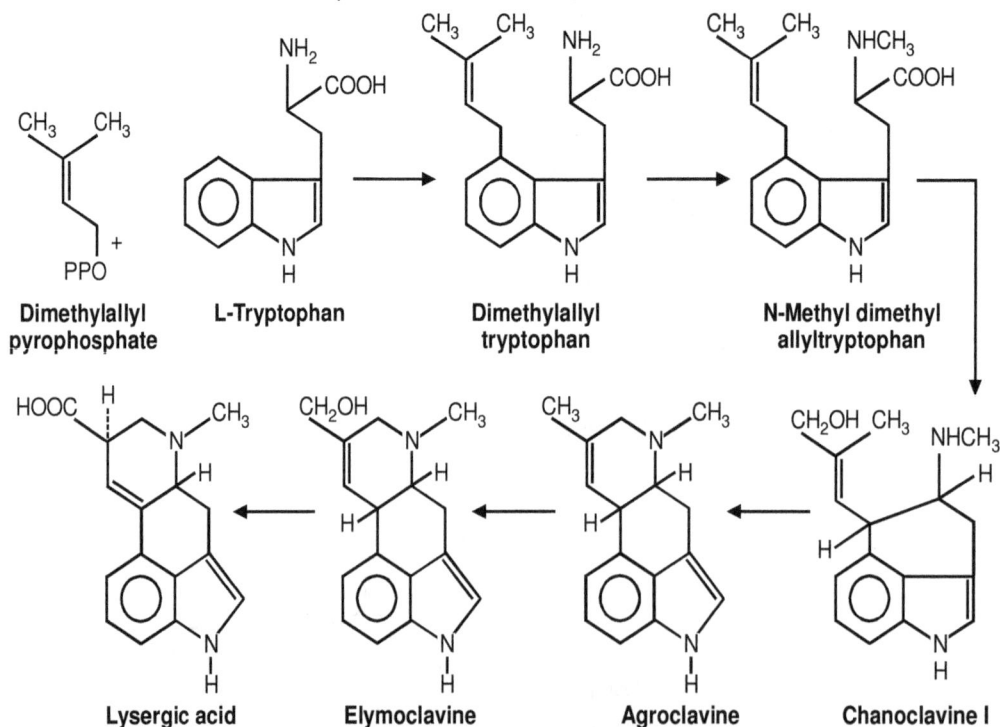

Dimethylallyl pyrophosphate

L-Tryptophan

Dimethylallyl tryptophan

N-Methyl dimethyl allyltryptophan

Lysergic acid

Elymoclavine

Agroclavine

Chanoclavine I

Biosynthesis of Lysergic acid

BIOSYNTHESIS OF ISOPRENOID COMPOUNDS

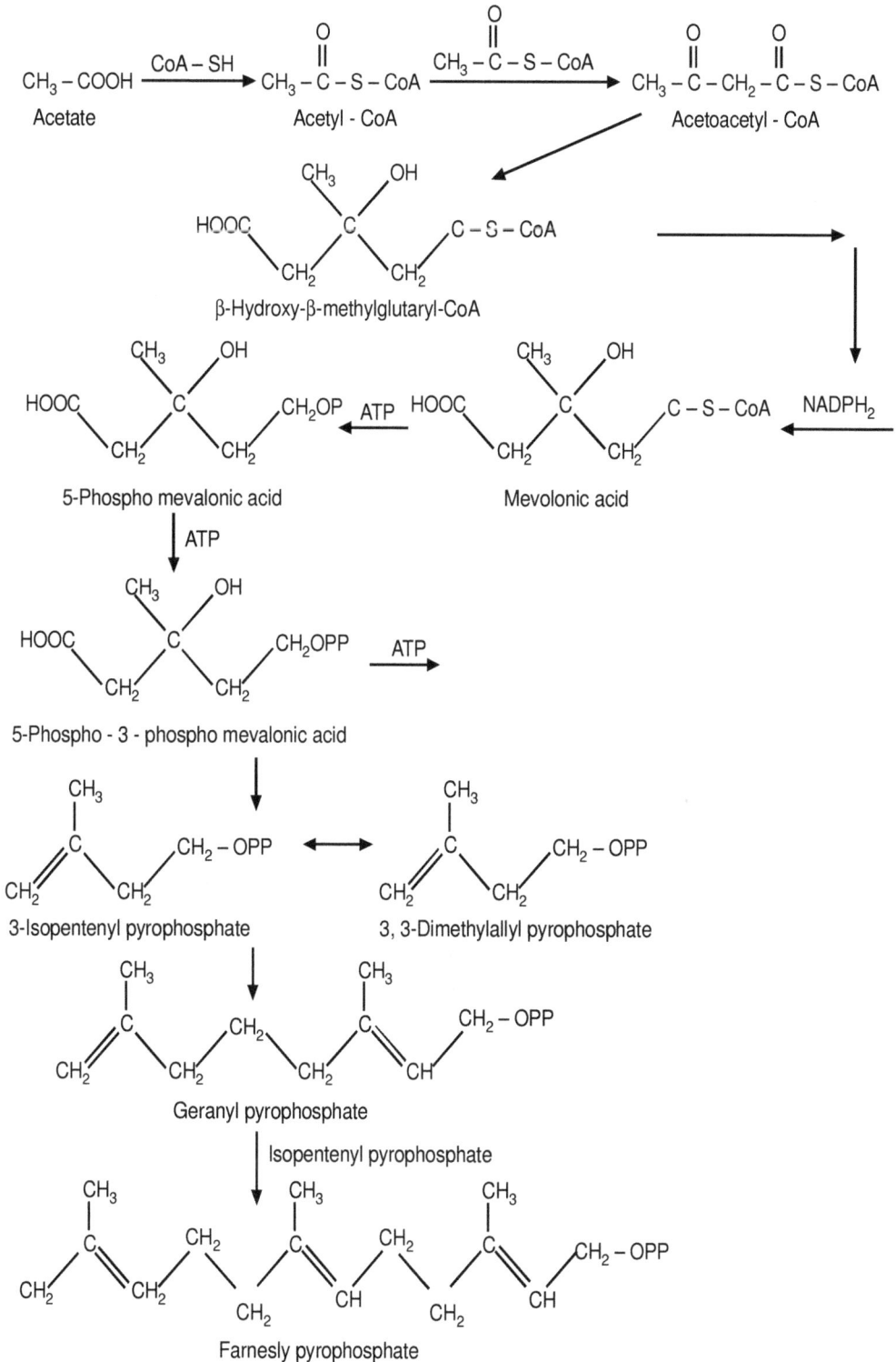

$CH_3 - COOH$ Acetate

$CH_3 - C - S - CoA$ Acetyl - CoA

$CH_3 - C - CH_2 - C - S - CoA$ Acetoacetyl - CoA

β-Hydroxy-β-methylglutaryl-CoA

5-Phospho mevalonic acid

Mevolonic acid

5-Phospho - 3 - phospho mevalonic acid

3-Isopentenyl pyrophosphate

3, 3-Dimethylallyl pyrophosphate

Geranyl pyrophosphate

Isopentenyl pyrophosphate

Farnesly pyrophosphate

The "biogenetic isoprene rule" as published by Ruziicka in 1953 is the basis for formation of various isoprenoid compounds. The discovery of mevalonic acid (3, 5-dihydroxy-3-methylavaleric acid) in 1956 and demonstration of its incorporation by living tissues into these compounds, to which the isoprene rule applied, were milestones in understanding biogenesis of terpene derivatives. It is established by research involving tracer techniques, inhibitor studies and ionophoresis that C_5 compound-isopentenylpyrophosphate is derived from mevalonic acid pyrophosphate by decarboxylation and dehydration. The C_{10} compound geranylpyrophosphate is formed by condensation of isopentenyl pyrophosphate with isomeric dimethylallylpyrophosphate. Further, C_6 units are added by participation of more isopentenylpyrophosphate units. From geranyl and farnesylpyrophosphates various isoprenoid structures are synthesized.

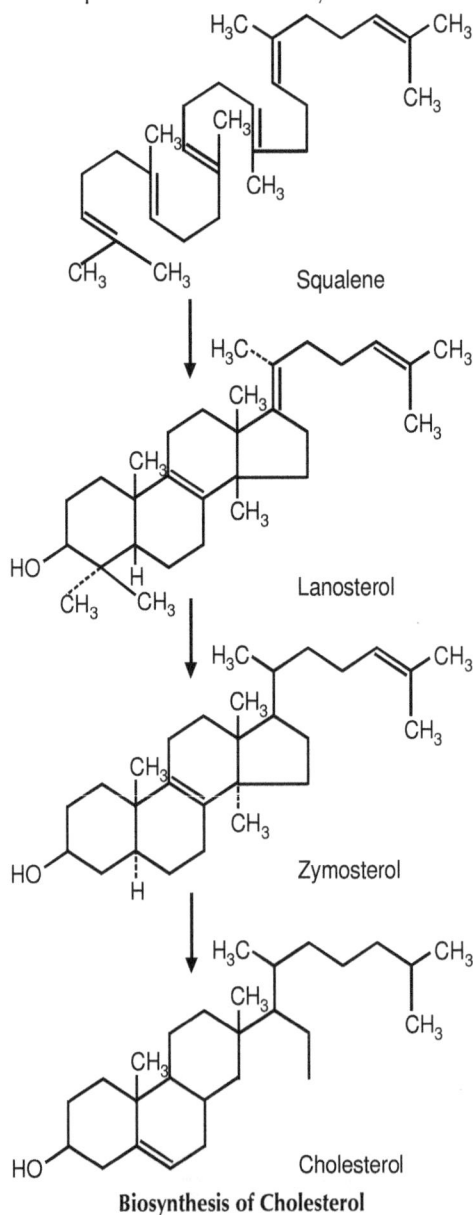

Squalene

Lanosterol

Zymosterol

Cholesterol

Biosynthesis of Cholesterol

Table 1.2: Biogenesis of Various Isoprenoid Compounds

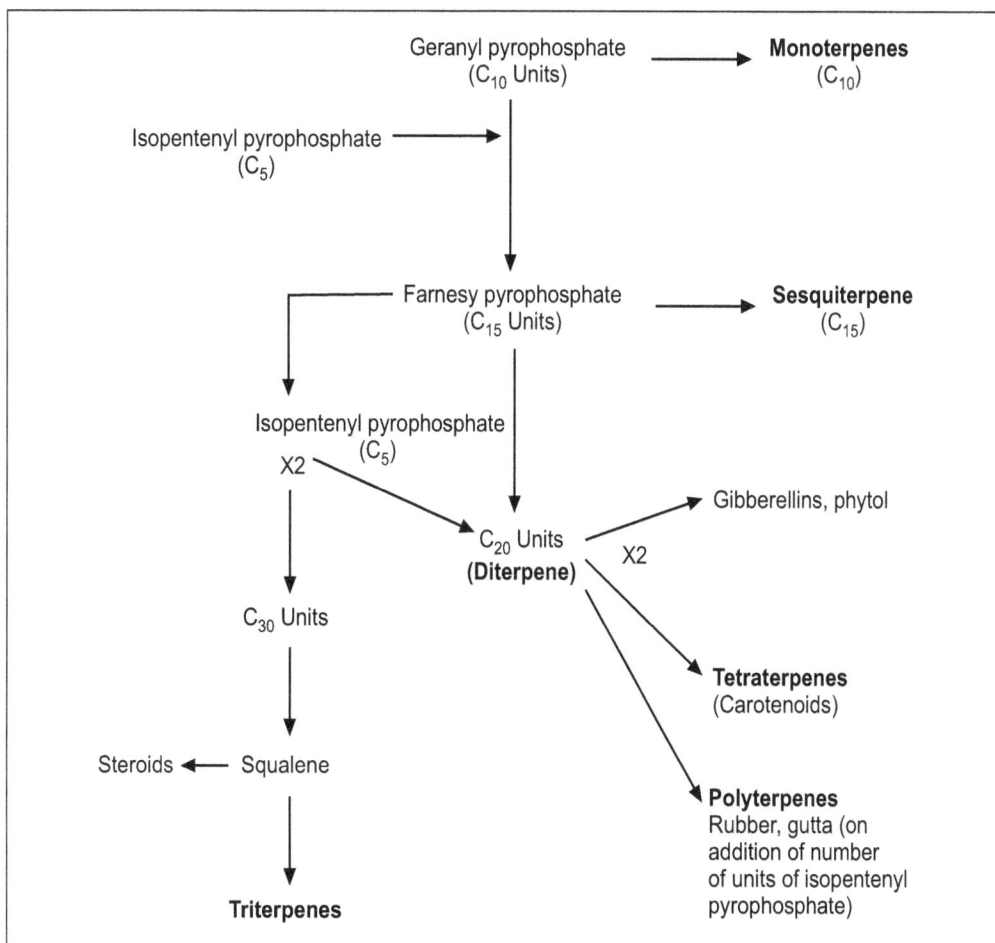

BIOSYNTHESIS OF TRIGLYCERIDES

It occurs in two stages. First stage is biosynthesis of fatty acid molecule while second stage is associated with formation of a triglyceride structure. For the formation of a fatty acid molecule, acetate is a precursor and reaction proceeds with presence of $NADPH_2$, Mn^{++}, ATP and two enzyme complexes (CoASH and Acetyl CoA) and carbon dioxide. Coenzyme A (CoA) comprises adenosine 3, 5 - diphosphate, pantothenic acid - 4 - phosphate and thioethanolamine. Acetyl CoA is the activated form of acetate moiety. The total reaction pathway is represented here.

This reaction occurs only in the formation of saturated fatty acids. In case of unsaturated, branched chain or other type of fatty acids, the biosynthetic pathways are not clearly known.

$$CH_3COOH + CoA-SH \xrightarrow{\text{ATP}} CH_3CO-S-CoA$$
Acetyl - CoA

$$Acetyl\text{-}CoA + CO_2 + ATP \xrightarrow[\text{Mn}^{++}]{\text{Biotin}}$$
$$\begin{array}{l} COOH \\ \diagup \\ CH_2 \\ \diagdown \\ CO-S-CoA \end{array}$$
Malonyl - CoA

$$CH_3CO-S-CoA + \begin{array}{l} COOH \\ \diagup \\ CH_2 \\ \diagdown \\ CO-S-CoA \end{array} \longrightarrow \begin{array}{l} COOH \\ \diagup \\ CH_3COCH \\ \diagdown \\ CO-S-CoA \end{array}$$
Malonyl - CoA   Intermediate + CoA – SH

↓ $NADP\,H_2$

$$CH_3-CH_2-CH_2-CO-S-CoA$$
Butyryl - CoA
$+ CO_2 + H_2O$

$$Butyryl\text{-}CoA + Malonyl\text{-}CoA \longrightarrow \begin{array}{l} COOH \\ \diagup \\ CH_3-CH_2-CH_2-CO-CH \\ \diagdown \\ CO-S-CoA \end{array}$$
Intermediate + $CO_2 + H_2O$

$$CH_3-CH_2-CH_2-CH_2-CH_2-CO-S-CoA + CO_2 + H_2$$
Caproyl - CoA

Caproyl - CoA + Malonyl - CoA ----------- chain goes on elongating to give
higher fatty acids.

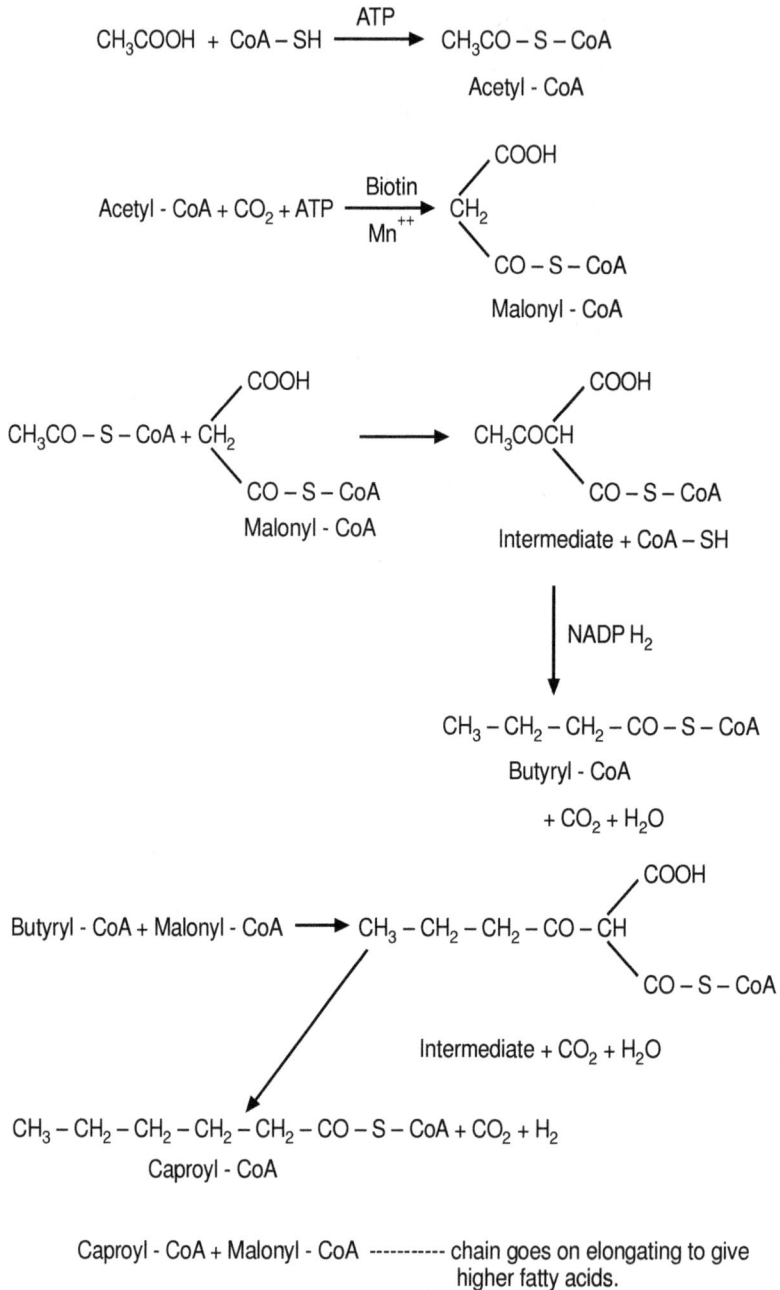

Second stage is the formation of triglyceride structure where required glycerol enters the reaction in the form of L – alpha – glycerophosphate while fatty acid comes as fatty acyl CoA.

$$CoA-S-CO-R \; + \; HO-\underset{\displaystyle \underset{\displaystyle CH_2-O\,\textcircled{P}}{|}}{\overset{\displaystyle \overset{\displaystyle CH_2OH}{|}}{CH}}$$

Fatty acyl - CoA

L - α - glycerophosphate

↓ CoA

$$CH_2OH-CO-R \\ | \\ HO-CH \qquad\qquad + \quad CoA-S-CO-R \\ | \qquad\qquad\qquad\qquad \text{Fatty acyl - CoA} \\ CH_2-O\,\textcircled{P}$$

L - α - lysophosphatidic Acid

↓ CoA

$$CH_2OCO-R \\ | \\ R-COO-CH \\ | \\ CH_2-O\,\textcircled{P}$$

L - α - phosphatidic Acid

↓

$$CH_2OCO-R \\ | \qquad\qquad\qquad + \;\; \text{Fatty acyl} - CoA \\ R-COO-CH \\ | \qquad\qquad\qquad\qquad CoA \\ CH_2OH \qquad\qquad\qquad\qquad CH_2OCO-R \\ \qquad\qquad\qquad\qquad\qquad\qquad | \\ \text{D - α, β - diglyceride} \qquad\qquad R-COO-CH \\ \qquad\qquad\qquad\qquad\qquad\qquad | \\ \qquad\qquad\qquad\qquad\qquad\qquad CH_2OCO-R$$

Triglyceride

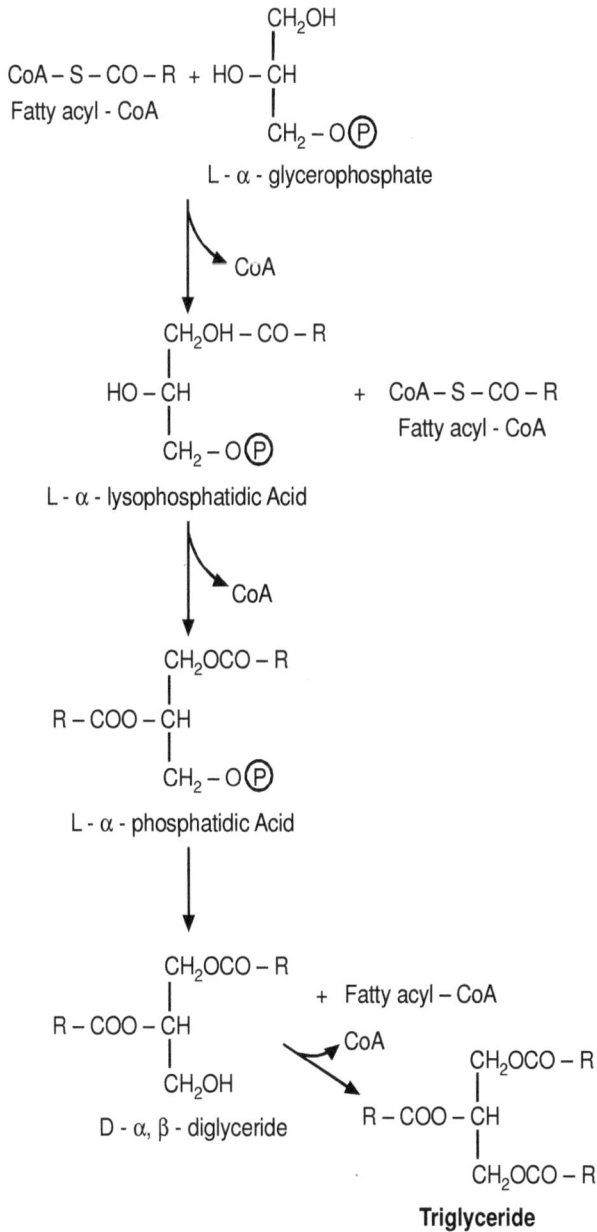

Depending on type of fatty acyl — CoA (value of R), simple or mixed glycerides are formed.

❖❖❖

Chapter 2

ALKALOIDS

Alkaloids are a chemically heterogeneous group of natural substances and comprise more than 6000 basic nitrogen containing organic compounds which occur in about 15 per cent of all vascular terrestrial plants and in more than 150 different plant families. The alkaloids exhibit diversity of structures and also show an extraordinary spectrum of pharmacological activities. Because of these characters, they are important for chemical, physiological, taxonomic and biogenetic studies.

HISTORY

The term 'alkaloid' or 'Pflanzenlkalien' was coined by **Meissner**, a German pharmacist, in 1819. The mankind has been using alkaloids for various purposes like poisons, medicines, poultices, teas, etc. The French chemist, **Derosne** in 1803, isolated narcotine. In the same year, morphine from opium was isolated by **Sertuerner**, a pharmacist of Paderborn near Hannover in 1803. **Pelletier** and **Calverton** from the Faculty of Pharmacy in Paris isolated emetine in 1817 and colchicine in 1819. This was followed by isolation of series of alkaloids from vegetable drugs, like strychnine (1817); brucine, piperine and caffeine (1819); quinine, colchicine and cinchonine (1820); coniine (1826); papaverine (1821) and thebaine (1835). By 1884, about 25 alkaloids were reported to be isolated from cinchona bark alone, but in 1870, a landmark in the domain of alkaloids was achieved by determining the structure of coniine which also became the first synthesized alkaloid in 1889. From the beginning of 19th century till date, it has proved to be a perpetual work to discover new alkaloids from plants and animals. In the present century, the proper structures were assigned to various alkaloids with the help of chromatographic and other sophisticated physical methods of analysis. As per a Russian review in 1973, the number of known alkaloids had reached up to 4959, amongst which, the structures of 3293 alkaloids were elucidated. At present, the number of alkaloids discovered has exceeded 6000.

Definition

In view of their chemical and physiological diversity, there is no comprehensive definition of alkaloids. The term is derived from the word 'alkali-like' and hence, they resemble some of the characters of naturally occuring complex amines. The term alkaloid also covers proto alkaloids and pseudoalkaloids. In view of all such variations, the only definition that brings all such compounds under one title is as follows: these are the organic products of natural or synthetic origin which are basic in nature and contain one or more nitrogen atoms, normally of heterocyclic nature, and possess specific physiological actions on human or animal body, when used in small quantities. The true alkaloids are toxic in nature, contain heterocyclic nitrogen which is derived from amino acids and always basic in nature. True alkaloids are normally present in plants as salts of organic acids. The 'proto alkaloids' or 'amino alkaloids' are simple amines in which the nitrogen is not in a heterocyclic ring. Some times, they are considered as biological amines. They are basic in nature and prepared in plants from amino acids. Some of the examples of these alkaloids are mescaline, N, N-dimethyl tryptamine, colchicine and ephedrine. The term 'pseudoalkaloids' includes mainly steroidal and terpenoid alkaloids and purines. They are not derived from amino acids. They do not show many of the typical characters of alkaloids, but give the standard qualitative tests for alkaloids. The examples of pseudoalkaloids are conessine and caffeine.

PROPERTIES

1. Physical Properties

With few exceptions, all the alkaloids are colourless, crystalline solids with a sharp melting point or decomposition range. Some alkaloids are amorphous gums, while others like coniine, sparteine, nicotine etc. are liquid and volatile in nature. Some alkaloids are coloured in nature, e.g. betanidin is red, berberine is yellow and salts of sanguinarine are copper red in colour.

In general, the free bases of alkaloids are soluble in organic non-polar, immiscible solvents. The salts of most alkaloids are soluble in water. In contrast, free bases are insoluble in water and their salts are also very sparingly soluble in organic solvents. The alkaloids containing quaternary bases are only water soluble. Some of the pseudoalkaloids and protoalkaloids show higher solubility in water. For example, colchicine is soluble in alkaline water, acid or water and caffeine (free base) is freely soluble in water. Quinine hydrochloride is highly soluble in water i.e. 1 part of quinine hydrochloride is soluble in less than 1 part of water, while only 1 part of quinine sulphate is soluble in 1000 parts of water.

The solubility of alkaloids and their salts is useful in pharmaceutical industry for the extraction and formulation of final pharmaceutical preparations.

2. Chemical Properties

Most of the alkaloids are basic in reaction, due to the availability of lone pair of electrons on nitrogen. The basic character of the alkaloidal compound is enhanced if the adjacent functional groups are electron releasing. The alkaloid turns to be neutral or acidic when the adjacent functional groups are electron withdrawing like amide group which reduces the availability of the lone pair of electrons. But, alkaloids exhibiting basic character are very much sensitive to decomposition and cause a problem during their storage. Their salt formation with an inorganic acid prevents many a time their decomposition.

The alkaloids may contain one or more number of nitrogen and it may exist in the form as primary ($R - NH_2$), e.g. mescaline; secondary amine ($R_2 - NH$), e.g. ephedrine; tertiary amine (R_3N) e.g. atropine; and quaternary ammonium compounds [R_4N^+X] e.g. tubocurarine chloride. In the last type, their properties vary from other alkaloids, owing to quaternary nature of nitrogen.

In the natural form, the alkaloids exist either in free state, as amine or as salt with acid or alkaloid N-oxides.

CHEMICAL TESTS FOR ALKALOIDS

The qualitative chemical tests used for detection of alkaloids are dependent on the characters of alkaloids to give precipitates as salts of organic acids or with compounds of heavy metals, like mercury, gold, platinum, etc.

The different reagents used are **Mayer's reagent** (potassium mercuric iodide solution) giving cream coloured precipitate; **Dragendorff's reagent** (potassium bismuth iodide solution) giving reddish brown precipitate; and **Wagner's reagent** (iodine-potassium iodide solution) yielding reddish brown precipitate. Some alkaloids also give yellow coloured precipitates with picric acid called as

Hager's reagent and picrolonic acid. Individual alkaloid gives colour or precipitate with certain specific reagent.

The chemical tests with heavy metals are not solely limited to alkaloids. Proteins, coumarins and α- pyrone also give precipitates with these reagents. It may be also noted that some alkaloids do not give such tests, like caffeine which is highly water soluble. Hence, the tests with heavy metals are in some cases false positive reactions or false negative reactions. For this purpose, the specific tests for individual alkaloids are more important for qualitative evaluation of crude drugs. These tests are covered under individual drugs.

ISOLATION AND EXTRACTION OF ALKALOIDS

The extraction of alkaloids is based on their basic character and solubility pattern. The normal procedures followed are to treat the moistened drug with alkali so as to set free the base as it exists in salt form and then to separate free base with organic solvent. This is known as *Stas Otto* process. Though the methods of extraction vary, generally following procedure is applied for small scale extraction of alkaloids. First, the plant is defatted with petroleum ether, especially in case of seed and leaf forms of drugs. Before applying this treatment, the alkaloid should be tested for its solubility in petroleum ether. Otherwise, the drug should be pretreated with acid to convert alkaloids into their salts. This happens in case of extraction of ergotamine from ergot. In the second stage, the drug may be extracted with polar solvents like water, ethanol, methanol, aqueous alcohol mixtures or with acidified aqueous solutions. By this treatment, the alkaloidal salts are transferred to polar solvent. It also helps in removing pigments, sugars and other organic secondary constituents. In the following stage, the alcohol solution is evaporated to thick syrup and is subjected to partition between aqueous acid solution and an organic solvent. After continuous extraction with organic solvent for some time, the aqueous phase is made alkaline with either sodium carbonate or ammonia. The basic aqueous solution is then extracted with convenient organic solvent followed by drying of alkaloid containing solution, normally with sodium sulphate, filtered and evaporated to yield alkaloid residue.

The other method meant for extraction of alkaloids employs the treatment of drug with ammonia so as to convert the alkaloidal salts into their free bases. Such liberated alkaloids in free base form are conveniently extracted with organic solvents like ether, benzene, chloroform, etc. The method is not useful for isolating alkaloids with quaternary nitrogen.

The further purification of crude extract of alkaloids is done by the following ways, which may, however, vary for individual alkaloid.

1. Direct crystallisation from solvent

It is a very simple method of isolation and may not be useful in case of complex mixtures.

2. Steam distillation

This method is specially employed for volatile liquid alkaloids like coniine, sparteine and nicotine, but otherwise this process is not suitable for alkaloids with high molecular weights.

3. Chromatographic techniques

This method has proved to be ideal for separation of a vast number of plant alkaloids. The different techniques of chromatography (thin layer, column, gas, liquid, ion exchange chromatography, HPTLC etc.) are used for separation of individual alkaloids from complex mixtures.

4. Gradient pH technique

Though alkaloids are basic in nature, there are variations in the extent of basicity of various alkaloids of the same plant. Depending on this character, the crude alkaloidal mixture is dissolved in 2 per cent tartaric acid solution and extracted with benzene so that the first fraction contains neutral and/or very weakly basic alkaloids. pH of the aqueous solution is increased gradually by 0.5 increments up to pH 9 and extraction is carried out at each pH level with organic solvent. By this way, the alkaloids with different basicity are extracted. Strongly basic alkaloids are extracted at the end. The general scheme for extraction of alkaloids can be summarized as follows.

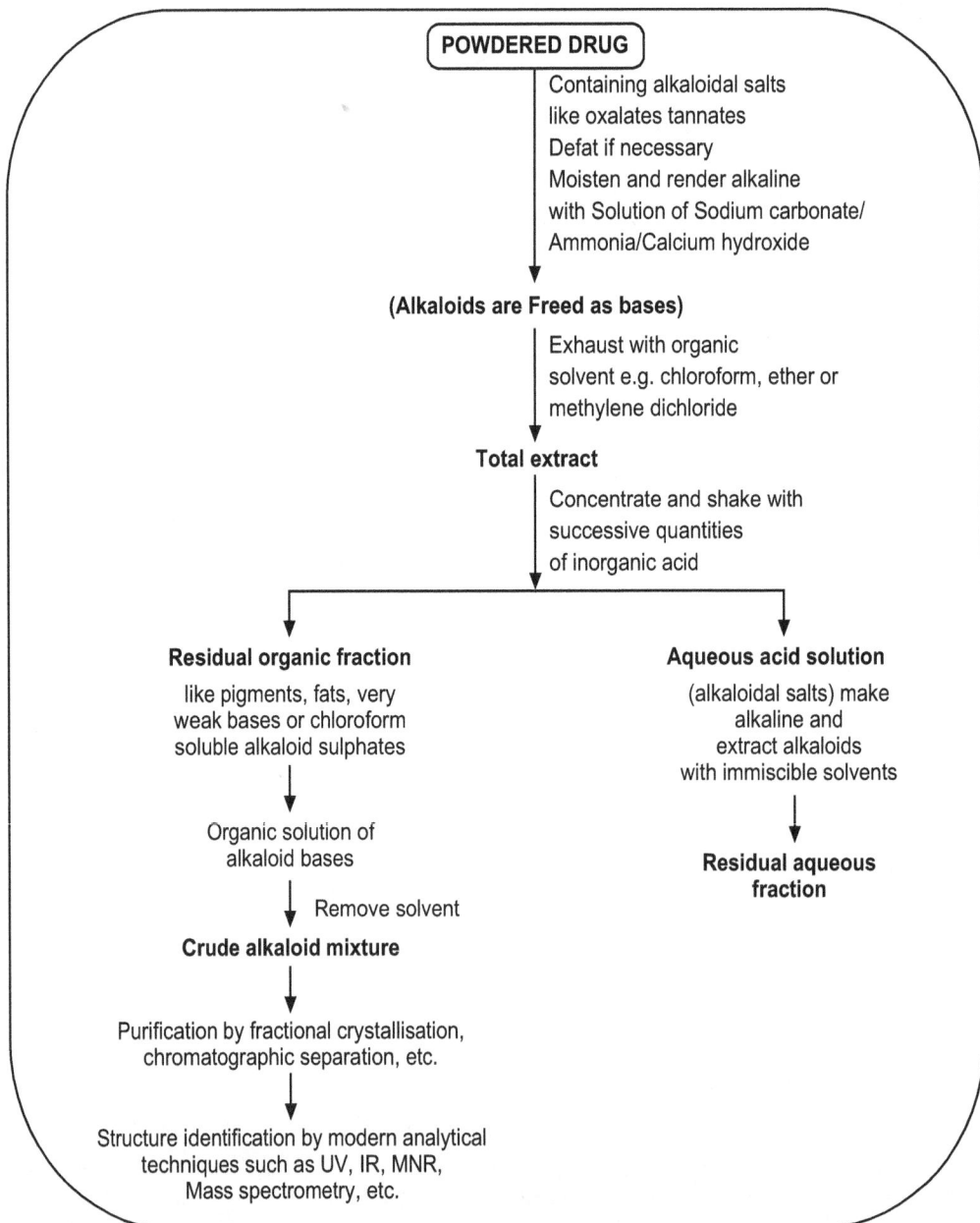

POWDERED DRUG

Containing alkaloidal salts
like oxalates tannates
Defat if necessary
Moisten and render alkaline
with Solution of Sodium carbonate/
Ammonia/Calcium hydroxide

(Alkaloids are Freed as bases)

Exhaust with organic
solvent e.g. chloroform, ether or
methylene dichloride

Total extract

Concentrate and shake with
successive quantities
of inorganic acid

Residual organic fraction

like pigments, fats, very
weak bases or chloroform
soluble alkaloid sulphates

Organic solution of
alkaloid bases

Remove solvent

Crude alkaloid mixture

Purification by fractional crystallisation,
chromatographic separation, etc.

Structure identification by modern analytical
techniques such as UV, IR, MNR,
Mass spectrometry, etc.

Aqueous acid solution

(alkaloidal salts) make
alkaline and
extract alkaloids
with immiscible solvents

**Residual aqueous
fraction**

CLASSIFICATION OF ALKALOIDS

The various methods proposed for classification of alkaloids are as follows:

1. **Pharmacological classification:** Depending on the physiological response, the alkaloids are classified under various pharmacological categories, like central nervous system stimulants or depressants, sympathomimetics, analgesics, purgatives, etc. This method does not take into account chemical nature of crude drugs. Within the same drug, the individual alkaloid may exhibit different action e.g. morphine is narcotic analgesic, while codeine is mainly antitussive. In cinchona, quinine is antimalarial, while quinidine is cardiac depressant.

2. **Taxonomic classification:** This method classifies the vast number of alkaloids based on their distribution in various plant families, like solanaceous or papillionaceous alkaloids. Preferably, they are grouped as per the name of the genus in which they occur, e.g. ephedra, cinchona, etc. From this classification, the chemotaxonomic classification has been further derived.

3. **Biosynthetic classification:** This method gives significance to the precursor from which the alkaloids are biosynthesized in the plant. Hence, the variety of alkaloids with different taxonomic distribution and physiological activities can be brought under same group, if they are derived from same precursor. e.g. all indole alkaloids from tryptophan are grouped together. The alkaloidal drugs are categorised on the fact whether they are derived from amino acid precursor as ornithine, lysine, tyrosine, phenylalanine, tryptophan, etc.

4. **Chemical classification:** This is the most accepted way of classification of alkaloids. The main criterion for chemical classification is the type of fundamental (normally heterocyclic) ring structure present in alkaloid.

The alkaloidal drugs are broadly categorised into two divisions:

(a) Heterocyclic alkaloids (True alkaloids) are divided into twelve groups according to nature of their heterocyclic ring.

(b) Non-hetero cyclic alkaloids or proto-alkaloids or biological amines or pseudoalkaloids.

The following chart indicates type of alkaloids and their occurrence in various plants along with basic chemical ring.

Table 2.1: A. Heterocyclic Alkaloids (True Alkaloids)

Type	Basic ring structure	Examples
1. Pyridine and Piperidine		Arecoline, anabasine, coniine, lobeline, pelletierine, trigonelline

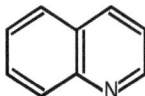

2.	Tropane (Piperidine N-methyl pyrrolidine)		Atropine, hyoscine, hyoscyamine, cocaine, pseudo- pelletierine, meteloidine
3.	Quinoline		Quinine, quinidine, cinchonine, cinchonidine cupreine, camptothecin.
4.	Isoquinoline		d-tubocurarine, berberine, emetine, cephaeline, papaverine, narcotine, narceine
5.	Indole or Benzopyrrol		Ergometrine, ergotamine, reserpine, vincristine, vinblastine, strychnine, brucine, physostigmine
6.	Imidazole or Glyoxaline		Pilocarpine, Isopilocarpine, Pilosine
7.	Steroidal (cyclopentano-perhydrophenanthrene ring) Alkaloids		Protoveratrine, solanidine, conessine, funtumine

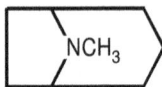

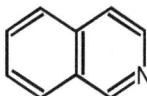

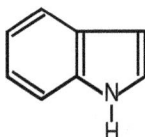

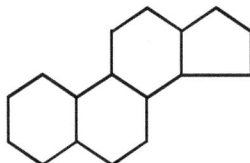

Amino – alkaloids

8.	Proto alkaloids		Ephedrine, pseudoephedrine. Mescaline, colchicine
9.	Purine Alkaloids (Pyrimidine/imidazole)		Caffeine, theobromine, theophylline

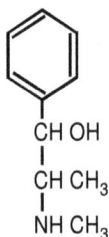

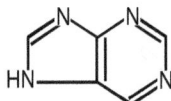

Table 2.1: B. Non-heterocyclic alkaloids Pseudo alkaloids

10. Diterpene Alkaloids		Aconitine, Aconine, hypoaconitine
11. Quinazoline Alkaloids		Vasicine and vasicinone

ROLE OF ALKALOIDS IN PLANTS

The alkaloids are poisonous in nature, but when used in small quantities, exert useful physiological effects on animals and human beings and hence they have secured significant place in medicine. Their exact role in nature and functions in the plants, if any, are still a topic of ambiguity. Only one aspect is clearly understood that they are synthesized by a particular, stereospecific, many a time complicated, and energy consuming pathways and further they are metabolized to other alkaloidal or non-alkaloidal substances. Some of the predicted roles of alkaloids in the plants are discussed below.

1. They are the reserve substances with an ability to supply nitrogen.

2. They might be the defensive mechanisms for plants growing in dry regions to protect from grazing animals, herbivores and insects.

3. It is also possible that they are end products of detoxification mechanism in plants, and by this way check formation of substances which may prove to be harmful to the plants.

4. They might have a possible role as growth regulatory factors in the plants.

5. They are present normally in conjugation with plant acids, like meconic acid, cinchotannic acid, etc. Therefore, alkaloids could be acting as carriers within plants for transportation of such acids.

OCCURRENCE AND DISTRIBUTION OF ALKALOIDS

The number of alkaloids discovered from plants has been continuously increasing. It is noted that alkaloids are of taxonomic importance. Their distribution in nature appears to be restricted or specific. Hence, the pattern of distribution of these compounds and their biological variability is of chemotaxonomic interest.

In general, the major distribution of alkaloids occurs in the angiosperms. But their presence is also detected in microorganisms, marine organisms, insects, animals and some of the lower plants. Some of the alkaloids reported from animal kingdom are castoramine from Canadian beaver, muscopyridine from musk deer and saxitoxin from "red tide". *Gonyaulax catenella* which has neurotoxic activity and a sex hormone which is a pyrrole derivative called 2, 3-dihydro - 7 methyl-1

H - pyrrolizin -1- one which occurs in many insects. It has been reported that among the bacteria, about 47 per cent species indicate the presence of alkaloids, e.g. pyocyanine from *Pseudomonas aeruginosa*. In the lower plants, although the alkaloids are found in less number, some important sources are ergot fungus giving peptide alkaloids, ergometrine, ergotamine, etc., lycopodine from lycopodium - a club moss, and also gymnosperms like ephedra alkaloids.

Out of the 60 different orders in higher plants, 34 orders contain alkaloids. Amongst them the prominent orders are Campanulales, Centrospermae, Gentianales, Geraniales, Liliflorae, Ranales, Rhoedales, Rosales, Rubiales, Tubiflorae and Sapindales.

The promising families with alkaloidal content are Amaryllidaceae, Apocynaceae, Berberidaceae, Euphorbiaceae, Leguminosae, Loganiaceae, Liliaceae, Lauraceae, Menispermaceae, Papaveraceae, Ranunculaceae, Rubiaceae, Rutaceae and Solanaceae. On the other hand, the orders like Curcurbitales, Fagales, Oleales, Salicales and the families like Labiatae and Rosaceae are practically devoid of alkaloids.

Within a plant, in most of the cases, the alkaloids are highly localized and concentrated in certain morphological parts only e.g. seeds (nux vomica, areca, physostigma), roots (rauwolfia, belladonna, ashwagandha), underground stems (sanguinaria), barks (kurchi, cinchona), leaves (coca leaf, lobelia, duboisia) and fruits (conium). In some cases, like vinca and ephedra, practically every part of plant contains alkaloids. The list of crude drugs containing alkaloids as active constituents is presented here.

Table 2.2: Types of alkaloids and crude drugs containing them

Sr. No.	Name of drug and synonym	Biological source	Active constituents	Uses
1. Pyridine-piperidine Alkaloids				
1.	Tabacco	Dried leaves of *Nicotiana tobacum* fam: Solanaceae	Nicotine, nor nicotine and anabusine	Not used medicinally quick acting poison.
2.	Areca (Betal nut)	Dried ripe seed of *Areca catechu*, Palmae	arecoline, arecaidine	respiratory stimulant
3.	Lobelia (Indian tobacco)	Dried leaves and tops of *Lobelia nicotianefolia*, Campanulaceae	lobeline, lobelanidine	respiratory stimulant
4.	Hemlock	Dried full grown but unfruits of Conium maculatum fam : Apiacene	Conine, N-methyl conine conhydrine	Sedative and antispasmotic very potent and poisonous.

Sr. No.	Name of drug and synonym	Biological source	Active constituents	Uses
2. Tropane Alkaloids				
5.	Belladonna (Deadly night shade Leaf)	Dried leaves and flowering tops of *Atropa belladonna*, Solanaceae	*l*-hyoscyamine, atropine	anticholinergic, antispasmodic
6.	Datura herb (Angel's trumpet)	Dried leaves and flowering tops of *Datura metel* var. *fastuosa*, Solanaceae	scopolamine, hyoscyamine, atropine	anticholinergic, in deodenal ulcers
7.	Hyoscyamus (Henbane)	Dried leaf and flowering top of *Hyoscyamus niger*, Solanaceae	*l*-hyoscyamine, hyoscine	anticholinergic, antispasmodic
8.	Stramonium (Thornapple leaves)	Dried leaves and flowering tops of *Datura stramonium*, Solanaceae	*l*-hyoscyamine, hyoscine, and atropine	anticholinergic, mydriatic, control motion, sickness
9.	Duboisia (Cork-tree)	Dried leaves of *Duboisia myoporoides*, Solanaceae	scopolamine	anticholinergic
10.	Coca	Dried leaves of *Erythroxylon coca*, Erythroxylaceae	cocaine, cinnamyl-cocaine, α-truxilline	local anaesthetic
3. Quinoline Alkaloids				
11.	Cinchona (Peruvian bark)	Dried root or stem bark of *Cinchona calisaya*, *C. officinalis*, *C. ledgeriana*, *C. succirubra*, Rubiaceae	quinine, quinidine, cinchonine, cinchonidine.	antimalarial, bitter tonic.
12.	Camptotheca (Cancer tree)	*Camptotheca acuminatal* Nyssaceae	Camptothecin	Antitumour

Sr. No.	Name of drug and synonym	Biological source	Active constituents	Uses
4. Isoquinoline Alkaloids				
13.	Opium (Raw opium)	Dried latex from the capsules of *Papaver somniferum*, Papaveraceae	narcotine, papaverine	narcotic analgesic, in diarrhoea
14.	Curare (South American arrow poison)	Dried extract of stems & leaves of various plants from family Loganiaceae and Menispermaceae	d-tubocurarine chloride	skeletal muscle relaxant
15.	Ipecacunha (Ipecac)	Roots and rhizomes of *Cephaelis ipecacuanha* and *C. acuminata* Rubiaceae	emetine, cephaeline	antiamoebic, emetic, expectorant
16.	Daruhaldi (Berberis)	Roots and rhizomes of *Berberis aristata*, and other *Berberis* species, Berberidaceae	berberine	astrigent in inflammation of mucous membranes
5. Indole/Benzopyrrole Alkaloids				
17.	Ergot (Ergot of Rye)	A fungal sclerotium of Claviceps purpurea Family Hypocraceae in ovary of rye plant Secale cereale. family Graminae	ergometrine, ergotamine	oxytocic, prevents postpartum haemorrhage; used in treatment of migraine
18.	Nux vomica (Crow Fig)	Seeds of Strychnos nux vomica, Loganiaceae	strychnine, brucine	CNS stimulant, bitter, stomachic, tonic
19.	Phyostigma (Calabar beans)	Seeds of Physostigma venonosum, Loganiaceae	Physostigmine, physovenine	cholinergic, (ophthalmic) in glaucoma
20.	Rauwolfia (Serpagandha)	Roots and rhizomes of Rauwolfia serpentina, Apocynaceae.	reserpine, rescinnamine	hypotensive tranquillizer
21.	Vinca (Catharanthus)	Entire plant of Catharanthus roseus, Apocynaceae	vincristine, vinblastine	anticancer (treatment of h odgkin's disease and leukemia)

Sr. No.	Name of drug and synonym	Biological source	Active constituents	Uses
6. Imidazole alkaloids				
22.	Pilocarus (Jaborandi)	Dried leaves of *Pilocarpus jaborandi,* Rutaceae	pilocarpine, pilosine	cholinergic (ophthalmic), used in treatment of glaucoma
7. Steroidal Alkaloids				
23.	Veratrum (white and green hellebore)	Dried rhizomes of *Veratrum album* and *V. viride,* Liliaceae	germidine, protoveratrine A and B	hypotensive, cardiac depressant
24.	Kurchi (Hollarrhena)	Dried bark of *Holarrhena antidysenterica,* Apocynaceae	conessine, isoconessine	antiamoebic
25.	Ashwagandha (Asgandh)	Dried roots of *Withania somnifera,* Solanaceae,	withanine, somniferine, withanolide (steroid)	sedative and also as antirheumatic
8. Amino Alkaloids (Proto-Alkaloids)				
26.	Ephedra (Ma-Huang)	Dried stems of *Ephedra gerardiana, E. equisetina, E. sinica etc.,* Ephedraceae	ephedrine, pseudoephedrine (alkaloidal amines)	sympathomimetic antiasthmatic, treatment of hay fever
27.	Colchicum (Meadow saffron seed)	Seed and corm of *Colchicum autumnale,* Liliaceae	Colchicine, demecolcine	treatment of gout, induction of polyploidy
28.	Gloriosa (Glory lily)	Dried rhizome & roots of *Gloriosa-superba,* Liliaceae	Colchicine	In the trearment of gout & cancer
9. Purine Alkaloids				
29.	Coffee	Dried ripe seeds of *Coffea arabica,* Rubiaceae	caffeine trigonelline	Stimulant, to counter effect over dosage of CNS depressant

Sr. No.	Name of drug and synonym	Biological source	Active constituents	Uses
30.	Cocoa seed (cocoa beans)	Seeds of *Theobroma cacao*, Sterculiaceae	theobromine, caffeine	diuretic
31.	Kola	Seeds of *Cola nitida* Sterculiaceae	caffeine, theobromine	CNS stimulant
32.	Tea (Thea)	Leaves and leaf buds of *Thea sinensis*, Theaceae	caffeine, theobromine	CNS stimulant and diuretic

10. Quinazoline alkaloids

33.	Vasaka (Adulsa)	Leaves of *Adhatoda vasica*, Acanthaceae	vasicine and vasicinone	Antitussives, expectorant

11. Diterpene alkaloids

34.	Aconite (Monkshood)	Dried roots of *Aconitum napellus*, Ranunculaceae	aconitine, neopelline	In treatment or rheumatism and sciatica

[1] PYRIDINE – PIPERIDINE ALKALOIDAL DRUGS

Reduced pyridine moiety is the base of these alkaloids. Tertiary base pyridine is reduced to secondary base piperidine. Examples are coniine, arecoline and ricinine. (a) Derivative of piperidine i.e lobeline from lobelia (b) derivative of pyridine : pyrrolidine, nicotine from tobacco (c) Derivative of nicotinic acid : Nacotine from tobacco.

TOBACCO

Biological Source

This consists of dried leaves of *Nicotiana tobacum*, belonging to family Solanaceae.

Geographical Source

Tobacco is cultivated on a commercial scale to a very large extent in China, United States and India. China produces annually 22 lacs metric tones, while India produces about 5 lacs metric tonnes of tobacco in a year. The other tobacco producing countries are Brazil, Russia, Turkey and Italy. In India, it is produced mainly in Andhra Pradesh, Gujrat, Karnataka, Orissa and Bihar.

Description

Tobacco, as a whole, is stout, ever green and viscid annual, 1 to 3 metres in height. It has thick erect stem and few branches. It bears about 20 leaves which are approximately 80 cm. in length. Flowers are light-red, white or pink in colour; fruits are capsules, elliptic, ovoid, 1.5 to 2.0 cm. in size. Seeds are spherical and 0.5 mm in diameter and brown in colour. Various varieties are known to be cultivated in India. Few of them are bidi tobacco, cigar tobacco, chewing and hookah tobacco.

Cultivation and Collection

Depending upon the type of tobacco, the requirements of soil and climate also vary. Warm climate, and well drained fertile land are favourable for its cultivation. Seeds are used for cultivation. The seeds are sown on the seed beds in winter or early spring. When the seedlings are about 12 weeks old, they are transplanted. In the flowering season, the flowering tops are cut so as to encourage the growth of foliage. Harvesting is done after 70 - 90 days of transplantation. The leaves are then subjected to processing by air curing, fire curing or fuel curing. During this process, the chemical changes occur and lead to development of flavour and aroma.

Macroscopic Characters (Fig. 2.1)

Colour   :   Green or slightly brown

Odour   :   Characteristic to Nicotine

Taste   :   Bitter

Size   :   60 - 80 cm. in length,   35 - 45 cm. in width

Shape   :   Ovate, elliptic or lanceolate

Fig. 2.1: Tobacco plant

Extra Features

The leaves are usually sessile, sometimes petiolate and with frilled wing.

Chemical Constituents

The tobacco contains pyridine-piperidine type of alkaloids, among which the most prominent is nicotine. The other alkaloids are nornicotine and anabasine.

Nicotine is colourless oily liquid and is readily soluble in water. Pure nicotine has an unpleasant smell of tobacco.

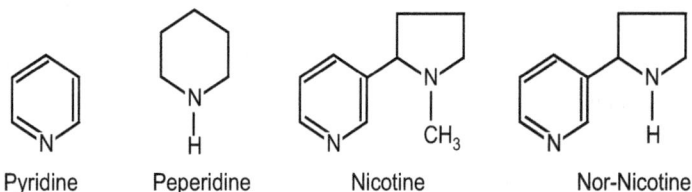

Pyridine   Peperidine   Nicotine   Nor-Nicotine

Uses

Nicotine exerts stimulant effects on heart and nervous system. It is not used medicinally. It is powerful quick acting poison. Even 40 mg. dose orallly is fatal to humans. It is not a drug is never prescribed by physicians. Rectified tobacco seed oil is used as edible oil in European countries. Nicotine is used in the manufacture of nicotinic acid and nicotinamide.

Tobacco and nicotine are known insecticides for last three centuries. Nicotine controls a wide range of insects. It is mainly used against soft bodied insects like aphides. It acts as a contact poison. It is also effective against white flies, moths, termites, butterfly-larvae, red-spider mites, etc. Nicotine is sprayed on crops in the form of nicotine sulphate. It has certain advantages over synthetic insecticides that it is safer, easier to handle and much less toxic to warm blooded animals. Because of its volatility, it evaporates earlier and leaves no harmful residue on the marketable products.

ARECA NUT

Synonym

Betel nut

Biological Source

These are the dried ripe seeds of *Areca catechu*, belonging to family Palmae. It should contain not less than 0.25 per cent of alkaloids, calculated as arecoline.

Geographical Source

Areca is cultivated in different parts of world such as India, Sri Lanka, South Eastern Asia, Philippines, East Africa, etc.

Macroscopic Characters (Fig. 2.2)

The plant of Areca is a tall palm which bears the fruits of nut type, each containing a single seed, thin seed coat and a large ruminant endosperm. The testa is deep-brown coloured and colourless exhibits a network of depressed, fawn coloured lines. The astringent seed is very hard and towards the flattened end, a small embryo is present.

Chemical Constituents

Areca contains a number of alkaloids, belonging to pyridine piperidine group and derived from amino-acid lysine. These alkaloids are reduced pyridine derivatives. The various alkaloids are arecoline, arecaidine, guvacine (tetrahydronicotinic acid) and guvacoline. Arecoline is methyl ester of arecaidine, while the latter is N-methylated derivative of guvacine. The drug also contains lipids, volatile oil, tannins and gum. Only arecoline possesses physiological activity.

Fig. 2.2: Areca plant with nuts

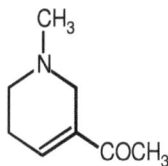

Arecoline

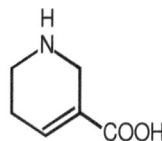

Guvacine

Standards

  (1) Foreign organic matter   - not more than 2 per cent

  (2) Ash   - not more than 5 per cent

  (3) Acid-insoluble ash   - not more than 2 per cent

Uses

Arecoline is parasympathomimetic. Areca has sialogogue properties and is consumed as masticatory in India and other eastern countries. But, the habit of chewing areca may cause oral leukoplakia. Areca is an anthelmentic drug and used as vermicide and taenifuge in veterinary practice. It is not used in human medicine.

LOBELIA HERB

Synonyms

Indian tobacco, Asthma weed, Lobelia herb.

Biological Source

It consists of the dried aerial parts of *Lobelia nicotianaefolia* Heyne, collected in October-November and dried in the shade. It belongs to family Campanulaceae.

Lobelia should contain not less than 0.55 per cent of total alkaloids, calculated as lobeline.

The other species viz. *L. inflata* is official in British Pharmacopoeia and United States Pharmacopoeia and consists of herbs of this species.

Geographical Source

It is a biennial or perennial herb growing on the Western Ghats of Maharashtra to Tryare in Kerala at an altitude of 700 to 2300 m. It is also found growing in South Maharashtra Nilgiri and in Karnataka. *Lobelia inflata* is indigenous to eastern and central U.S.A. and Holland.

History

The name of this drug has been derived to honour a botanist Matthias de L'obel. Cutler described its utility in asthma in 1813 and Reece introduced this drug in 1829 to English medical profession.

Cultivation, Collection and Preparation

Lobelia IP is collected from wild sources, while Lobelia BP/USP is collected both from wild and cultivated varieties. Lobeline, the major alkaloid of this drug is obtained by synthesis also.

Macroscopic Characters (Fig. 2.3)

Colour -   Stems are green with purplish tinge

Odour -   None

Taste -   Extremely acrid and irritating

Size -   The total height of the plant is about 2 to 3 m.

The plants have rounded or somewhat angular stems. They are usually branched at the top and slightly pubescent and hollow. Lobelia stems bear alternate leaves which are oblong lanceolate, sub-sessile and finely serrulate. The upper leaves are shorter and the lower leaves are bigger in size. The leaves are 5 to 25 cm in length, and 1 to 5 cm in breadth. Flowers are white with 3 lobes, terminal recemes are from 30 to 100 cm in length. Fruits are bilocular inflatted capsules which are sub-globose, about 5 to 10 cm in diameter and with longitudinal ribs. Seeds are small, ellipsoidal and compressed.

Fig. 2.3: Lobelia Flowering Herb

Chemical Constituents

Lobelia contains 0.5 to 1.2 of total alkaloids, important of them is lobeline. Lobelidine, Lobelanine, isolobelanine and lobelanidine are the other alkaloids present in the drug. It also contains pungent volatile oil, resin, gum and fixed oil.

Lobeline	R_1 = H, OH,	R_2 = O	
Lobelanine	R_1 = O,	R_2 = O	
Lobelanidine	R_1 = H, OH,	R_2 = H, OH	

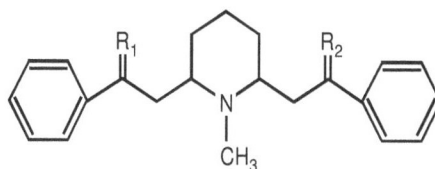

Lobeline $C_{22}H_{27}O_2N$ occurs as colourless crystals and soluble in hot alcohol. It forms hydrobromide, hydrochloride and methiodide salts.

Nobel prize winner **H.O. Weiland** and co-workers have been credited with the structural determination of lobelia alkaloids.

Chemical Tests

1. Solution of lobeline in sulphuric acid gives red colour with formaldehyde.

2. Lobeline solution on boiling produces acetophenone which is recognised by smell.

Uses

Lobelia is mainly used in the treatment of asthma and as respiratory stimulant. It is used for bronchial asthma and chronic bronchitis. Previously, the fumes of powdered lobelia were used for inhalation. It is also claimed that lobelia is useful as a smoking deterrent. In parenteral form, lobeline hydrochloride is given for resuscitation of new born infants, through umbilical vein.

Lobeline has similar physiological effects as that of nicotine.

It is a cardiovascular stimulant having the effects through carotid chemoreceptors. Cough and pain receptors are stimulated by lobeline.

HEMLOCK

Synonyms

Poison Hemlock, Spotted hemlock, Poison pursley.

Biological Source

This consists of dried full grown but unripe fruits of the plant *Conium maculatum* family Apiaccae (Umbelliferae).

Geographical Source

It is native of temperate regions of Europe, West Asia and North Africa. It has been naturalized in Australia. North America and New Zealand. It is found on drained soils, near streams, ditches and other waste places.

Cultivation and Collection

Hemlock fruits are collected from wild grown plants only, when they are fully grown, but before they ripen i.e. before they change their colour from green to yellow fruits are dried thoroughly and stored.

Macroscopic Characters

Hemlock is a biennial plant reaching the hight of 1.5 – 2.5 metres, stems are hollow green in colour and are usually spotted or streaked with red or purple on lower half of the stem.

Fig. 2.4: Hemlock herb

Leaves are roughly triangular and about 50 × 40 cm in size. Flowers are small white and in umbels from 10 to 15 cm across.

Fig. 2.5: Fruity top of Hemlock

Microscopic Characters

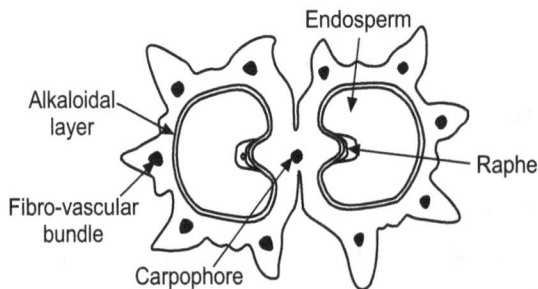

Fig. 2.6: T.S. of Hemlock Fruit (cremocarp)

Chemical Constituents

Pyridine-piperidinic, alkaloids are the active constituents of hemlock. About eight alkaloids have been reported and are named as coniine, N-methyl coniine, conhydrine, pseudo conhydrine and gamma-conicrine. Coniine is a liquid and volatile alkaloid. Their actions are similar to Nicotine. All parts of plant contain alkaloids but maximum in fruits from 0.05 – 2.5 per cent. Hemlock also contain volatile oil and fixed oil.

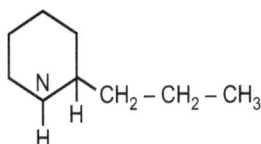

Coniine

Chemical Test

Crush the dried fruits and add dilute solution of pot. hydroxide. Strong mouse-like odour is developed (due to liberation of coniine alkaloid).

Action of Mechanism

The alkaloid coniine disrupts the working of central nervous system through action on nicotinic acetylcholine receptors. Alkaloids are highly potent and even in small doses cause respiratory collapse and even death. The death is due to blocking the neuromuscular junction similar to curare, due to lack of oxygen to heart and brain. Overdoses produce paralysis and loss of speech, depression and respiratory system and then death.

Uses

Hemlock is highly potent and very poisonous, needs to be used with lot of care.

Poison hemlock has been used as sedative and anti-spasmodic.

[2] TROPANE ALKALOIDAL DRUGS

Tropane molecule represents the fusion of pyrrolidine and piperidine ring with common methylated nitrogen. The alkaloids containing with methylated tropane nucleus are chemotaxonomic characters of family Solanaceae. Out of 10-12 such alkaloids of this family, therapeutic value is present only in *l*-hyoscyamine. Hyoscine and racemic form of hyoscyamine viz. atropine. They have anticholinergic effects. They are employed for different purposes. Hyoscyamine is used in parkinsonism. Hyoscine is useful as preanaesthetic in surgery and also in motion sickness. Atropine is employed to achieve paralysis of parasympathetic nerves like in treatment of eye diseases.

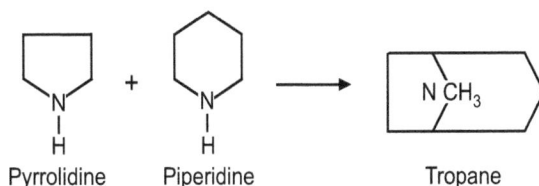

Pyrrolidine   Piperidine   Tropane

Family Solanaceae includes 72 genera, out of which only 8 genera viz. *Datura, Atropa, Duboisia, Hyoscyamus, Scopolia, Physoclaina, Mandrogora* and *Solandra* contain *l*-hyoscyamine, hyoscine and atropine. The species, with such alkaloids, under these genera are grouped in the following way.

1. Hyoscyamine as main alkaloid: *Datura stramonium, Atropa belladonna, A. acuminata, Duboisia myoporoides* (South Australian Strain).

2. Hyoscine as main alkaloid: *D. metel, Duboisia myoporoides* (North Australian Strain)

3. Hyoscyamine and Hyoscine (both in low quantities): *Hyoscyamus niger, Mandrogora officinarum.*

BELLADONNA HERB

Synonyms

Belladonna Leaf; Belladonnae Folium; Deadly night shade leaf (European belladonna).

Biological Source

Belladonna herb consists of dried leaves or the leaves and other aerial parts of *Atropa belladonna* Linn. (European belladonna) or *Atropa acuminata* Royle ex-Lindley (Indian belladonna) or mixture of both the species collected when the plants are in flowering condition. It belongs to family Solanaceae. It contains not less than 0.3 per cent of the alkaloids of belladonna herb, calculated as *l*-hyoscyamine.

Geographical Source

It is indigenous to and cultivated in England and other European countries. In India, it is found in the Western Himalayas from Simla to Kashmir and adjoining areas of Himachal Pradesh. Its chief habitat is Jammu and in forests of Sindh, and Chinab valley.

History

Because of the hallucinogenic effect of this plant, it was used as witch craft in the middle ages. In ancient times, the juice of this plant was used as a cosmetic, because of its dilatory effect on the pupil of the eye. This drug was first introduced in the London Pharmacopoeia in 1809.

Cultivation and Collection

Cultivation of belladonna at an altitude of 1400 m above the sea level is found to be satisfactory, if proper irrigation facilities are provided. It is observed that the yield per hectare can be increased substantially by proper cultivation technology. The experimental trials of applications of several fungicides and insecticides right from the treatment of the seeds up to the foliar sprays were very encouraging. Its cultivation in Jammu and Kashmir is found to be successful.

Belladonna berries are crushed to get the seeds for cultivation. Proper processing like washing and sieving is performed. Only healthy seeds are used for cultivation. Seeds are sown by broadcasting method in well prepared beds with the application of fungicide like diathon. Sowing is done in May and July. The seedlings are ready for transplantation by theend of September.

Transplanting is done by keeping certain distance between two plants and the seedlings are irrigated carefully. Fertilizers like urea, potash and superphosphate are given as per the needs. Insecticidal sprays like sevin are also tried when the plant reaches maturity. The leaves, as well as, the flowering tops are cut and sundried or dried in shade. During drying, care is taken to retain the green colour. While grading and packing for market, woolly stems and foreign organic matter are rejected. The yield per hectare is found to be 200 to 600 kg.

Macroscopic Characters (Fig. 2.7)

Colour   -   Leaves - Green to brownish-green

                    Flowers - Purple to yellowish-brown

                    Fruits - Green to brown

Odour   -   Slight and characteristic

Taste   -   Bitter and acrid

Size   -   Leaves - 5 - 25 cm long and 2.5 - 12 cm wide

                    Flowers - Corolla 2.5 cm long and 1.5 cm wide

                    Fruits - About 10 cm in diameter.

Shape   -   Leaves - Ovate, lanceolate to broadly ovate, with acuminate apex, decurrent lamina, entire margin, petiolate, brittle and transversely broken.

                    Flowers - Campanulate, 5, small reflexed lobes of corolla.

                    Fruits - Berries, sub-globular in shape with numerous flat seeds.

Fig. 2.7: Belladonna Herb

Extra Features

In general, the entire drug is seen as crumpled and twisted. The dropping flowers are associated with as many pairs of leaves. The flowers are with 5 stamens, superior bilocular ovary with numerous seeds.

Microscopic Characters (Fig. 2.8)

Epidermal cells with slightly sinuous anticlinal wall and striated cuticle, anisocytic stomata and occasionally uniseriate multicellular covering trichomes are present. There are glandular trichomes which are uniseriate and with unicellular heads. The palisade ratio is 5 to 7.

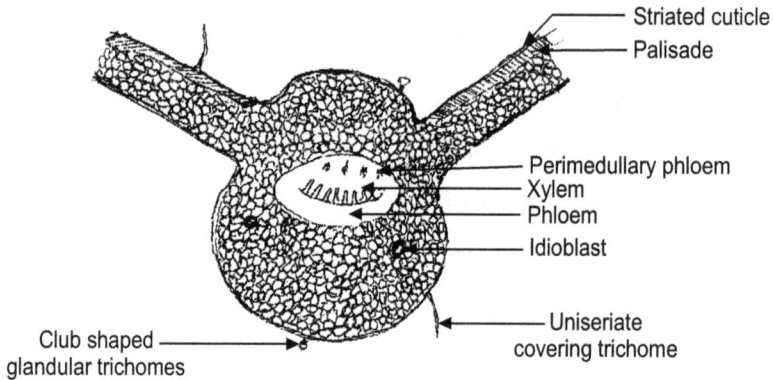

Fig. 2.8: T. S. of Belladonna Leaf

Chemical Constituents

The total alkaloidal content of drug is 0.4 - 1 per cent and varies in different parts of plant, roots (0.6 per cent), stems (0.05 per cent), leaves (0.4 per cent), unripe and ripe berries (0.19 - 0.21 per cent) and seeds (0.33 per cent).

The main alkaloids are *l*-hyoscyamine and its racemic form atropine. The drug also contains belladonine, scopoletin (*l* - methyl aesculetin), hyoscine, pyridine and N - methyl pyrroline. The later two are the volatile bases. Homotropine is a synthetic compound and is preferred in the medical profession as the synthetic process of atropine and hyoscyamine is very costly.

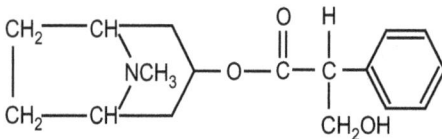

Atropine (Tropine (±) - Tropate)

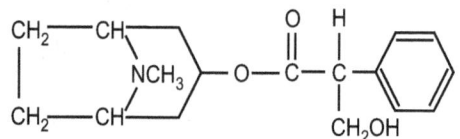

Hyoscyamine (Tropine (−) - Tropate)

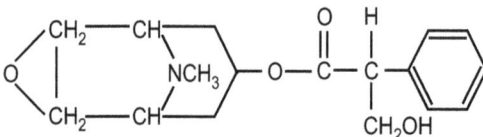

Hyoscine (Scopalamine)

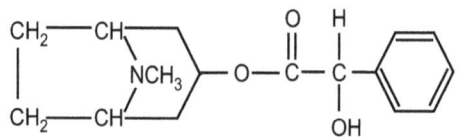

Homotropine

Standards

1. Total ash　　　　　　　　　- 14 per cent
2. Acid-insoluble ash　　　　　- 3 per cent
3. Foreign organic matter　　　- not more than 3 per cent

It gives Vitali - Morin reaction　- positive

Uses

It is the parasympatholytic drug with anticholinergic properties. It is used to reduce the secretions such as sweat, saliva and gastric juice and also to reduce spasm in cases of intestinal gripping due to strong purgatives. It is also used as an antidote in opium and chloral hydrate poisoning.

Dose

0.6 to 1 ml in the form of belladonna tincture - 4 times a day.

DATURA

Synonyms

Datura herb, Angel's trumpet.

Biological Source

Datura consists of the dried leaves and flowering tops of *Datura metel* and *D. metel* var. *fastuosa* Safford. It belongs to family Solanaceae.

It should contain not less than 0.20 per cent of total alkaloids of Datura, calculated as *l*-hyoscyamine.

Geographical Source

It is found in India, England and other tropical and subtropical regions.

Cultivation and Collection

The drug is cultivated by sowing the seeds. The germination is normally very slow. If the seeds are soaked in water and kept overnight, the rate of germination increases. About 7 - 8 kg of seeds per hectare are required for sowing purpose. The seeds require about 15 - 20 days for germination. Weeding and thinning are necessary and performed when are 10 - 15 cm tall. The distance kept in between 2 plants is about 75 - 100 cm. The plants should be supplied with organic fertilizers and proper irrigation. The drug is collected after 4 months of its cultivation. The leaves and branches are removed, drug is dried in the sun and marketed by packing in gunny bags.

Macroscopic Characters (Fig. 2.9)

The drug has a characteristic but unpleasant odour and a bitter taste. The drug contains entire, broken wrinkled, crushed leaves along with stem fragments and floral parts. The entire leaf has length of 9 - 18 cm and width of 8 - 13 cm. Normally, the margin is of entire, but in some cases sinuated with rounded or acute 2 - 4 broad lobes. The leaf is covered with minute hairs, lower surface is slightly pale in colour and the leaf has a thin texture. The leaf is unequal at the base with acute apex and glabrous lamina. Each leaf has 3 - 4 coarse veins on each side and 4 - 6 secondary veins on either side of the midrib. Flowers are reddish-purple on outer side and whitish on inner side. Corolla is thin, acuminate, triangular to circular in shape. Flowers are funnel shaped with pedicel which is never erect. The stems, as well as, branches of drug are purple coloured. Brown coloured seeds are triangular and are found in the thorny capsule.

Fig. 2.9: *Datura metel* in Fruiting Stage

Microscopic Characters (Fig. 2.10)

Through the transverse section, it shows its dorsiventral character. The epidermal cells of both sides show anisocytic or cruciferous stomata. The cells are covered with thin cuticle and glandular and non-glandular simple trichomes. About 40 per cent of the lamina is occupied by single layer of palisade cells. Approximately 6 - 8 layers of spongy parenchymatous cells are present. The midrib shows vascular tissue with protoxylem and metaxylem. Trichomes are more on the midrib region. Stomatal index is 12.7 - 19.5 for upper surface and 21.2 - 24 for lower surface. Palisade ratio is 3.5 - 6.5. The spongy parenchyma contains calcium oxalate crystals.

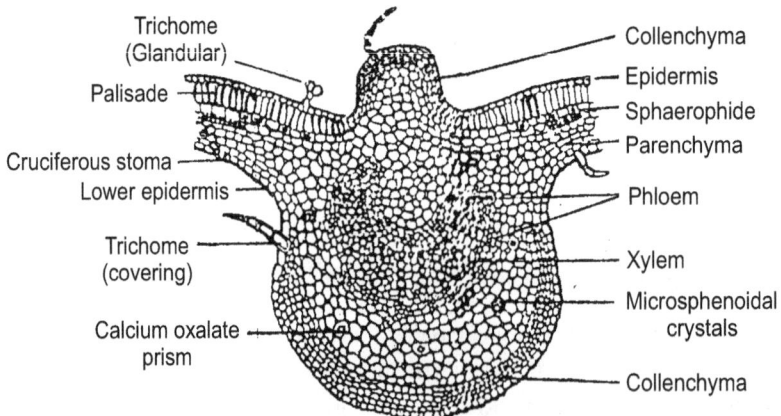

Fig. 2.10: T.S. of Datura leaf

Chemical Constituents

Datura herb contains upto 0.5 per cent of total alkaloids, among which hyoscine (scopolamine) is the main alkaloid, while *l*-hyoscyamine (scopoline) and atropine are present in very less quantities (see belladonna herb).

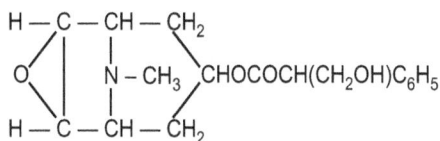

$$H-C-CH-CH_2$$
$$O \overset{|}{\underset{|}{\diamondsuit}} \quad N-CH_3 \quad CHOCOCH(CH_2OH)C_6H_5$$
$$H-C-CH-CH_2$$

Scopalamine

Hyoscine ($C_{17} H_{21} O_4 N$) is an ester of tropic acid and scopine. It is the principal alkaloid of *Datura*, *Scopolia* and *Duboisia* species. The occurrence of hyoscine is restricted only to Solanaceae family.

Standards

1. Stems, flowers, fruits　.- not more than 20 per cent
2. Foreign organic matter - not more than 2 per cent
3. Acid-insoluble ash　　- not more than 4 per cent

Chemical Test (Vitali-Morin reaction)

1. The tropane alkaloid is treated with fuming nitric acid, followed by evaporation to dryness and addition of methanolic potassium hydroxide solution to an acetone solution of nitrated residue. Violet coloration takes place due to tropan derivative.

2. On addition of silver nitrate solution to solution of hyoscine hydrobromide, yellowish white precipitate is formed, which is insoluble in nitric acid, but soluble in dilute ammonia.

Uses

Datura herb and its main alkaloid hyoscine are parasympatholytic with anticholinergic and central nervous system depressant effects. The drug is used in cerebral excitement. Along with morphine, it is used as preoperative medication. It is also used in treatment of asthma and cough.

Hyoscine hydrobromide is used in motion sickness, gastric or duodenal ulcers.

HYOSCYAMUS

Synonyms

Henbane, Hyoscyamus herb, Hyoscyamus leaves.

Biological Source

It consists of the dried leaves, or leaves and flowering tops of *Hyoscyamus niger*, belonging to family Solanaceae.

It should contain not less than 0.05 per cent of alkaloids of hyoscyamus, calculated as *l*-hyoscyamine. It is grown as a biennial herb.

Geographical Source

Hyoscyamus is a native of Western Asia, North Africa, Europe and India. It is cultivated in Russia, Belgium, Hungary and India.

History

Hyoscyamus is known since ancient times and was used as household drug. Dioscorides has also mentioned about this drug in his literature. The references about this drug are found in 'Arabian Nights' and also in Anglo-Saxon works on medicine. The drug was reintroduced in 1809 in the London Pharmacopoeia.

Cultivation and Collection

The cultivation is done in temperate region at an altitude of 2400 to 3300 m. The drug is cultivated on commercial scale in England, Egypt, U.S.S.R., and Hungary. In India, it is cultivated in Kashmir to a limited extent. The method of propagation is by seeds. The small seed beds are raised and seeds are sown. The seeds require about two weeks for germination. The seedlings are transplanted in field in the month of May by keeping a distance of half metre between them and about 75 cm between two rows. The plants are kept free of weeds and occasional hoeing is also done. The crop is harvested when it reaches maturity. Under all favourable conditions, the yield of the drug per hectare is 1000 kg - 1500 kg.

Macroscopic Chracters (Fig. 2.11)

The fresh drug has characteristic and strong odour with a bitter and acrid taste.

The leaves have about 25 cm long lamina and they are pale greyish green in colour. The shape is ovate-oblong to triangular ovate. In few cases, they may contain short petiole, otherwise they are sessile. The margin has acute triangular lobes, which are irregularly dentate. The apex is acute, the lamina is covered with glandular hair. There is the prominent midrib with pinnate venation. The flowers are funnel shaped and yellow in colour, showing purplish veins.

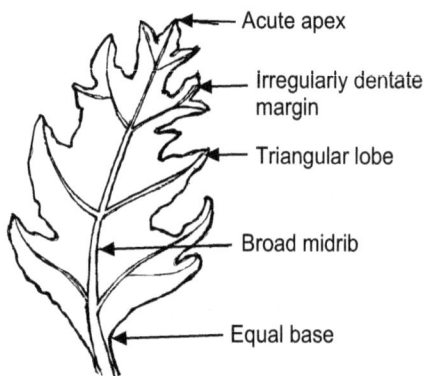

Fig. 2.11: Hyoscyamus Leaf

Microscopic Characters (Fig. 2.12)

The leaf is dorsiventral. Epidermis is covered with smooth cuticle and numerous glandular trichomes. Anisocytic stomata are present in epidermal layer. Palisade cells are present in a single layer but all cells contain prismatic or cluster crystals of calcium oxalate. Near the veins, some times, the idioblasts are present containing microspheroidal crystals. Midrib shows many bicollateral vascular bundles arranged in an arc.

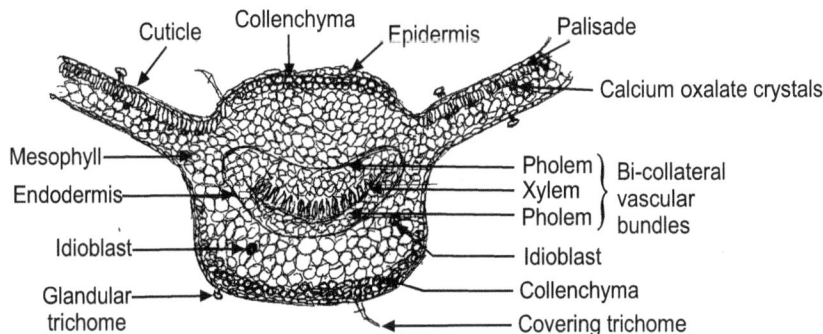

Fig. 2.12: T.S. of Hyoscyamus leaf

Chemical Constituents

The total alkaloids present in the drug range from 0.05 - 0.15 per cent in which about 75 per cent is hyoscyamine. Atropine and hyoscine are present in fewer amount. The alkaloidal percentage is more in petiole than in the stem or lamina.

The principal alkaloid of this drug (–) hyoscyamine ($C_{17}H_{23}NO_3$) is an ester of tropic acid and tropine, and is more active than the racemic form i.e. atropine. During the extraction, it is racemized to atropine (see belladonna herb).

Chemical Tests

It gives Vitali-Morin test positive in case of datura herb.

Uses

It is used to counteract gripping due to purgatives and also to relieve spasms of urinary tract. It is also sedative and used to check salivary secretion. It is an expectorant too. It is an antispasmodic and antiasthmatic.

Dose

Hyoscyamine sulphate - 125 - 250 mg, 3 - 4 times a day.

WITHANIA

Synonyms

Withania root, Asgandh, Winter cherry, Ashwagandha.

Biological Source

It consists of dried roots and stem bases of *Withania somnifera* (Linn.) Dunal, belonging to family Solanaceae and should contain not less than 0.02 per cent of total withanolide A and withaferin A on dried basis.

Geographical Source

This plant grows wildly in all dry parts and subtropical India. It occurs in Madhya Pradesh, Uttar Pradesh, Punjab plains and North Western parts of India like Gujarat and Rajasthan. It is also found in Congo, South Africa, Egypt, Morocco, Jordan, Pakistan and Afghanistan.

Cultivation, Collection and Preparation

It is reported that the plants from different sources vary in their morphological and therapeutic properties. Now-a-days, the cultivation is mainly done in Madhya Pradesh (Manasa plantations), where, about 2000 hectares are under cultivation. The propagation is done by seeds, for which about 4 - 5 kg of seeds are required per hectare. The seeds are sown in the soil which is unsuitable for other crops. The sowing is done towards June-July and during growth, no special arrangements are made for irrigation. Even the nitrogenous fertilizers lead to formation of small roots, but large foliage. Towards December or January, the plants bear flowers and fruits and during January, harvesting is initiated which lasts upto March. The roots are collected by uprooting the plant and either entire roots or the pieces thereof are dried immediately.

Macroscopic Characters (Fig. 2.13)

The roots show buff to grey yellow outer colour with longitudinal wrinkles. They are unbranched, straight, conical and some of them bear a crown. The root crown possesses a number of bud scars. Roots are bitter in taste and fresh roots smell similar to urine of horse (hence ashwagandha). The fracture is smooth and powdery.

Microscopic Characters

The transverse section of root shows exfoliated cork which is non-lignified with 2 - 4 layers of phellogen and about 15 - 20 rows of phelloderm. It prominently shows parts of vascular tissue like cambium, consisting of 3 - 5 layers of tangentially elongated cells, phloem region with parenchyma, sieve tubes and companion cells. Secondary xylem is hard which forms a continuous vascular ring interrupted by medullary rays. The transverse section of stem base shows pith, pericyclic fibres, xylem with tracheids, fibres, and starch grains.

Fig. 2.13: Ashwagandha plant Roots

Chemical Constituents

The main constituents of ashwagandha are alkaloids and steroidal lactones. Among the various alkaloids, withanine is the main constituent. The other alkaloids are somniferine, somnine, somniferinine, withananine, pseudo-withanine, tropine, pseudo tropine, 3-α-gloyloxytropane, choline, cuscohygrine, isopelletierine, anaferine and anahydrine. Two acyl steryl glucosides viz. Sitoindoside VII and sitoindoside VIII have been isolated from roots.

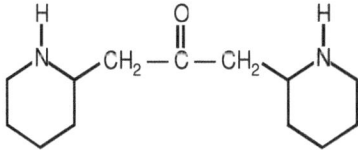 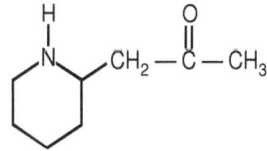

Anaferine   **Dl-isopelletierine**

The leaves contain steroidal lactones, which are commonly called as "withanolides". The withanolides have C_{28} steroidal nucleus with C_9 side chain, having six membered lactone rings. Lavie et.al, have isolated such compounds from plants grown in Israel, India and S. Africa.

The various withanolides reported are as on the next page.

Steroids (withanolides) of Ashwagandha

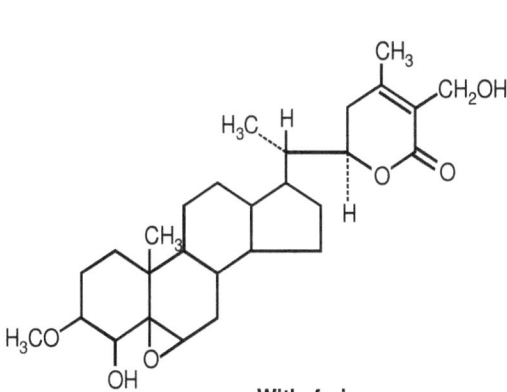

Withaferin

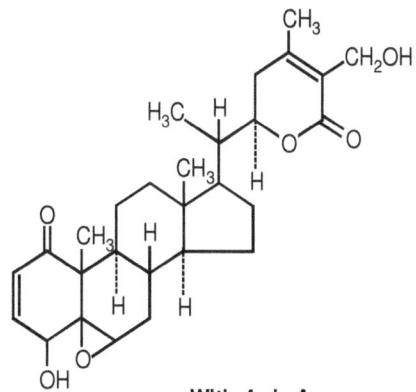

Withaferin A

These compounds have been obtained from *W. somnifera* chemotype I.

Another series of steroidal lactones viz. withanolide E to M have been obtained from chemotype III.

The drug also contains two monohydric alcohols called somnitol and somnirol; withanic acid; a phytosterol and ipuranol; and a mixture of fatty acids containing cerotic acid, oleic acid, palmitic acid and stearic acid.

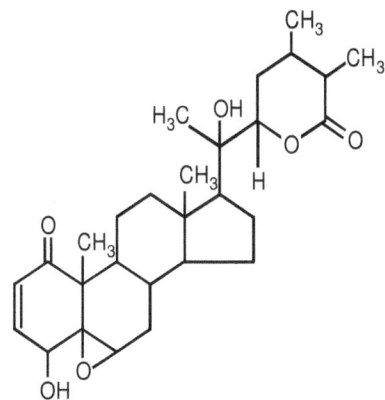

Withanolide A

Standards

    (1) Foreign organic matter   - not more than 2 per cent

    (2) Total ash   - not more than 7 per cent

    (3) Acid-insoluble ash   - not more than 1.2 per cent

    (4) Alcohol soluble matter   - not less than 16 per cent

Uses

Ashwagandha has sedative and hypnotic effects. It has hypotensive, respiratory, stimulant actions alongwith bradycardia. It is an immuno-modulatory agent. Sitoindoside (VII and VIII) have been shown to possess anti-stress activity. It acts as mood stabilizer revives mind and body.

Traditionally, it has been used in the treatment of rheumatism, gout, hypertension, nervine and skin-diseases. This drug prevents bony degenerative changes in arthritic conditions. It has been widely used as sex stimulant and rejuvenator and is considered as strength and vigour promoting drug especially in geriatric cases.

The leaf extracts shows activity against *Staphylococcus aureus* and *Ranikhet virus*.

DUBOISIA

Synonyms

Cork wood, Cork tree.

Biological Source

Duboisia consists of the dried leaves of *Duboisia myoporoides* R. Brown, and *D. leichhardtii*. It belongs to family Solanaceae.

Geographical Source

It a Australian herb found around Sydney along the coastal area tablelands of North Quinceland, New South Wales and New Caledonia island.

Macroscopic Characters

Duboisia is perennial shrub up to 3.0 metres in height with brown to purple colour bark on young stage while a corky older bark at later stage

Leaves are 3-10 cm into 1-2 cm. Leaves are tapering at both the ends and alternatively arranged.

Colour is pale green.

Taste is intensely bitter.

Fig. 2.14: Duboisia herb

Chemical Constituents

Duboisia is considered as the chief commercial source of scopolamine and atropine. It contains *l*-hyoscyamine which is converted to atropine during extraction. Along with it, the drug also contains nor-hyoscyamine, tigloidine, valtropine, tiglyoxytropine.

The synthetic process for scopolamine and atropine is very costly and hence, much reliance is placed on its natural source.

Atropine ($C_{17}H_{23}O_3N$) occurs as colourless crystals, with a bitter taste and no odour. It is soluble in chloroform and alcohol. It is a racemic form of hyoscyamine.

Chemical Test

1. The addition of gold chloride solution to atropine in water and hydrochloric acid gives' lemon yellow precipitate.

2. It gives positive Vitali Morin reaction.

Uses

Duboisia leaves are the main source of atropine and scopolamine.

Atropine is the parasympatholytic drug. It also causes stimulant action on central, medullary and higher nerve centres. Atropine has many different therapeutic uses. It is used as an antidote for pilocarpine, physostigmine and other choline esters. It relieves bronchial spasms in asthma. As it suppresses the gastric secretions, it is used in peptic ulcer. It has applications in ophthalmic practice, because of its dilatory effects on pupil of the eye. It is also used to reduce tremor and rigidity in parkinsonism.

COCA LEAVES

Synonym

Coca

Biological Source

These are the dried leaves of *Erythroxylon coca* and *Erythroxylon truxillense*, belonging to family Erythroxylaceae.

Commercially, *E. coca* is known as Bolivian or Huanuco coca and *E. truxillense* is known as Peruvian or Truxillo coca.

Geographical Source

It is native to South American countries like Peru and Bolivia. Commercially, it is cultivated in Java, Peru, Bolivia, Columbia, Sri Lanka and India.

History

Since ancient times, the coca leaves have been used by South Americans as a masticatory and were reserved for only native chiefs and Incas. It was considered as 'divine plant'. The first report about coca leaves was prepared by **Monardes** in 1569. The plant was brought to Europe in 1688. Cocaine was isolated in 1860 and its local anaesthetic effects were discovered in 1882 by **Koeller** from Vienna. It was introduced into medicine some time in the later half of nineteenth century.

Cultivation, Collection and Preparation

Coca leaves contain the tropane alkaloids, mainly cocaine. Though it has local anaesthetic effects, it has hallucinogenic actions, leading to addiction. Because of this, all activities about this plant are strictly governed by Narcotic Drugs and Psychotropic Substances Act 1985 in India and by relevant acts in other countries.

Coca plant is mainly cultivated in Java, Peru and Bolivia. The open fields at an altitude of 500 - 2000 metres are suitable for cultivation of this drug. Propagation is done by sowing the seeds in nursery beds. The seedlings on attaining a height of about 15-20 cm are transplanted to open fields by keeping a distance of 2 metres. A thatched roof is provided in initial days of cultivation. The height of the plant is maintained upto 2 metres by regular prunning. The drug is collected over a 'period of 3 years, at an interval of one year. The leaves are collected in dry weather and dried in the shed or by artificial means.

From the crude cocaine obtained from leaves, the pure cocaine is isolated. The total alkaloids are hydrolysed to get ecgonine, from which cocaine is synthesised. Large scale manufacture of cocaine is mostly done in U.K, where the processes are protected by patents.

Macroscopic Characters [Figs. 2.15 (a) and 2.15 (b)]

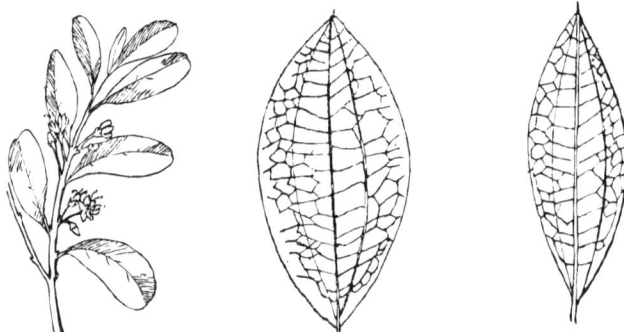

Fig. 2.15 (a): *Erythroxylum coca* herb and leaf　　**Fig. 2.15 (b): A leaf of *E. truxillense***

Peru variety gives the elliptical leaves which are 1.5 - 5 cm long with very thin texture and pale green colour. Bolivian variety contains greenish-brown leaves, which are oval in shape and measure 2.5 - 7.5 cm in length and 1.5 - 4 cm in width. It bears a prominent midrib. In Bolivian variety, the lower surface shows two curved lines, one each on both sides of midrib.

Both the varieties have a characteristic odour with a bitter and aromatic taste.

Microscopic Characters (Fig. 2.16)

Microscopically, both the varieties have similar characters. They are isobilateral leaves and show presence of parenchyma under both epidermal layers. Midrib is typical and is partly encircled by considerable amount of collenchyma. The lower epidermis shows presence of papillae and numerous paracytic stomata. The drug

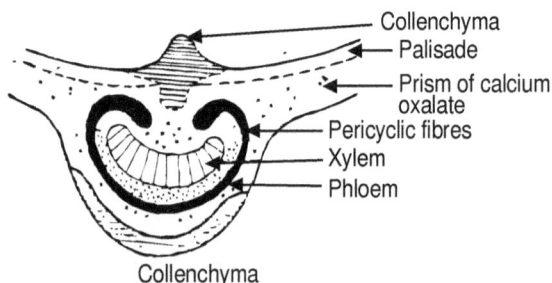

Fig. 2.16: Coca Leaf in T.S.

does not show trichomes, but some of the cells of epidermis contain mucilage. Numerous lignified idioblasts are present near the veins. Starch grains, stone cells and rarely calcium oxalate crystals are present in epidermal cells.

Chemical Constituents

The drug contains 0.7 - 1.5 per cent of total alkaloids. The majority of alkaloids are tropane esters. Both Peruvian and Bolivian coca contain less alkaloids, but higher proportion of cocaine among them. Java coca has higher percentage (upto 2 per cent) of alkaloids, but low amount of cocaine.

The coca plant yields the tropane derived alkaloids such as cocaine (methyl benzoyl ecgonine), cinnamyl cocaine (methyl cinnamoylecgonine), α-truxilline (methyl - α - truxilloylecgonine), tropocaine, benzoyltropine, dihydroxytropane and benzoylecgonine.

In commerce, the price of leaves is determined on the basis of ecgonine content, because it is converted synthetically into commerical cocaine. In this process, ecgonine is obtained from crude alkaloids which are first isolated by treatment with lime and organic solvents or dilute sulphuric acid. All free bases may be converted to their hydrochlorides. Further, they are hydrolysed by boiling with dilute hydrochloric acid. Due to this, the different bases liberate ecgonine in following way.

Cinnamyl cocaine → ecgonine + methyl alcohol + cinnamic acid
Cocaine → ecgonine + methyl alcohol + benzoic acid
α - truxilline → ecgonine + methyl alcohol + α - truxillic acid

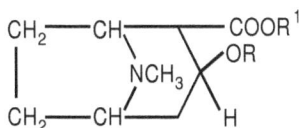

Ecgonine Derivatives

R	R'	Name of Alkaloid
H	H	Ecgonine
CH_3	$C_6 H_5 CO$ (benzoyl)	Cocaine
H	CH_3	Methylecgonine
H	$C_6 H_5 CH = CHCO$ (cinnamoyl)	Cinnamoylecgonine
H	$C_6 H_5 CO$	Benzoylecgonine

Ecgonine liberated from all the alkaloids is obtained as its hydrochloride. It is further converted to benzoylecgonine by treating with benzoic anhydride. The benzoylated base is next treated with methyl iodide and sodium methoxide in methyl alcohol by which methylation occurs and brings out cocaine i.e. methyl benzoyl ecgonine. This synthetic cocaine is isolated as cocaine hydrochloride.

Chemical Test

Cocaine powder is treated with sulphuric acid, heated, followed by addition and mixing of water. It gives the characteristic smell of methyl benzoate.

Uses

Cocaine is a local anaesthetic. It is the first known local anaesthetic from which various other synthetic substitutes with similar activity have been prepared.

In general, coca leaves are used as stimulant, restorative and also in convulsions. Cocaine reduces the sedative and respiratory depressant effects of morphine and allied drugs, due to CNS stimulant properties.

Owing to hallucinogenic and addictive effects of cocaine, it has become the drug of abuse and hence, its uses are limited to ophthalmic surgery and surgery of ear, nose and throat.

[3] QUINOLINE ALKALOIDAL DRUGS

CINCHONA

Synonyms

Jesuit's bark, Peruvian bark

Biological Source

It is the dried bark of the cultivated trees of *Cinchona calisaya* Wedd., *C. ledgeriana* Moens, *C. officinalis* Linn, *C. succirubra* Pav. ex-klotzsch, or of hybrids of either of the last two species with either of the first two. Cinchona belongs to family Rubiaceae. It contains not less than 6 per cent of total alkaloids of cinchona.

Geographical Source

India, Bolivia, Columbia, Ecuador, Peru, Tanzania, Guatemala, Indonesia and Sri Lanka are the countries where cinchona is found. In India, it is cultivated in Annamalai hills (Coimbatore district) and Nilgiri hills (Nilgiri district) in Tamil Nadu and in Darjeeling area of West Bengal.

History

Cinchona is native to Eastern slopes of the Andes at high altitudes (1500 - 2500 metres). It is known that the bark was first used as an antipyretic in 1630 by Jesuits, although it was discovered in 1513 in Peru. Owing to the efforts of Viceroy of Peru, Count Chinchon it was introduced as a drug in Europe around 1655. It was officially reported as an infusion in London Pharmacopoeia in 1677. In the honour of viceroy, the genus was described by Linnaeus as Cinchona in 1742. After the isolation of quinine and cinchonine in 1820 by Pelletier and Canventon, the alkaloids or their mixtures came into use as a medicine. In 1860, *C. calisaya, C. micrantha* and *C. succirubra* were introduced in India by Markham. Dutch, introduced *C. ledgeriana* in Java and sooner the country became world's most important source for this drug with a high alkaloidal content. In India, owing to the antimalarial and antipyretic use of this drug; right from 1880, a large area was taken for cultivation of cinchona in West Bengal, which eventually shifted to South India.

Cultivation, Collection and Preparation

Most of the cinchona species profusely grow in sub-tropical or tropical climates at a height of about 1000 - 3000 metres. The trees, growing below this height are found to have less percentage of quinine. The rainfall conditions required are uniform (from 250 - 380 cm in a year). The favourable growth is achieved between an atmospheric temperature of 60° - 75°F. Cinchona requires light, well drained forest soil which is rich in organic matter. The acidic soil having a pH of 4.2 - 5.6 and a small amount of nitrogen are found to be most favourable for growth. Cinchona needs slopping situation, high humidity and protection from wind.

The propagation is done with either seeds or budding or layering. In West Bengal, only budding is practised and in Tamil Nadu, the budding and layering methods are applied. The seeds of cinchona are very small and light in weight. About one gramme of cinchona seeds contain 3500 seeds. They are admixed with soil during sowing. The maintenance of genetic purity causes a problem as high cross fertilization occurs in cinchona plants. This affects the yield, like in high alkaloid content giving species, such as C. ledgeriana, the average alkaloid content is reduced. The seeds should be immediately used for propagation as on storage they lose their viability. The germination takes place in 3 - 6 weeks. The seedlings with 2 pairs of leaves are transplanted and space of 6 - 10 cm is maintained inbetween two seedlings and 2 rows. The young seedlings are protected from direct sunlight. In forest soil, they are transplanted after 15 months of growth and preferably before heavy rainfall. A distance of 2 × 2 metres is maintained between two plants. As cinchona consists of stem, as well as root bark, the plants from 4 - 20 years of age are selected for harvesting, but the maximum alkaloidal content is found to 6 - 10 years old plants. The bark is collected by coppicing method. For this purpose, vertical incisions are made on branches, trunk of tree and these incisions are connected by horizontal circles. The bark is then stripped off and dried in sun light and further by artificial heat. The drying is done below 175°F. During drying, the bark loses up to 70 per cent of its weight. The care should be taken to avoid molding or fermentation during drying. The quills of drug are packed in gunny bags and marketed. The root bark is collected by uprooting the trees and bark is separated manually.

During the two world wars, Java and Indonesia lost their positions as potential producers of cinchona. After that, India has gained the prime position as producer and supplier of cinchona and quinine. By 1985 - 86, the production had reached upto 10 lakh kg of bark and about 26,000 kg of quinine salts.

India exported quinine and its salts of ₹ 299.0 lacs during 1995-96.

Extraction of Quinine

For extraction of quinine, the bark is powdered and extracted with benzene or toluene in presence of alkali. Further, the alkaloids are extracted with dil. sulphuric acid. By bringing the acid extract to neutrality, quinine sulphate separates, as it is sparingly soluble.

Macroscopic Characters (Fig. 2.17)

Cinchona bark has a slight and characteristic odour, but somewhat astringent and intensely bitter taste. In general, the bark is available in the form of quills and curved pieces.

Flowering bunch of Cinchona   Piece of Cinchona Bark

Fig. 2.17

Stem bark: It is up to 30 cm in length and about 2 to 6 mm in thickness. The outer surface shows dull brown grey or grey colour and many a time, shows presence of mosses and lichens owing to its growth in heavy rainfall areas. The bark is rough and has transverse fissures. These fissures are different in different species. It is furrowed or wrinkled longitudinally. The outer bark in some varieties shows exfoliation. The inner surface is pale yellowish-brown to deep reddish-brown and the colour depends on the species. The fracture is short in external layers and fibrous in the inner portion.

Root bark: It occurs in length of 2 - 7 cm. The bark is curved, twisted or irregularly channelled. The outer and inner surfaces are similar in colour. The outer surface is scaly and shows depressions. The inner surface is striated.

The different commercial varieties have some special characters. *C. succirubra* is also called as red bark, while *C. ledgeriana* is referred to as yellow bark. *C. robusta* is the hybrid between *C. succirubra* and *C. officinalis*.

Table 2.3: The typical characters of 4 main species of cinchona

Characters	C. calisaya	C. ledgeriana	C. officinalis	C. succirubra
Size	Diameter is from 12 - 25 mm and thickness from 2 - 5 mm	Diameter is 12-25 mm and thickness varies from 2 - 5 mm	Diameter is upto 12 mm and thickness is upto 1.5 mm	Diameter is from 20 - 40 mm and thickness from 2 - 5 mm
Other features	Broad longitudinal fissure with transverse cracks.	Broad longitudinal fissures and cracks more in number, but less deep. Some pieces show longitudinal wrinkles and reddish warts	It shows a number of transverse cracks	Well marked longitudinal wrinkles, but less number of transverse cracks. Only some pieces show reddishwarts
Powder	Cinnamon brown	Cinnamon brown	Yellow	Reddish brown

Microscopic Characters (Fig. 2.18)

Cinchona exhibits the typical histological characters of the bark. The cork cells are thin-walled, followed by phelloderm. The cortex consists of several secretory channels and phloem fibres. Medullary rays with radially arranged cells are present. Idioblast of calcium oxalate is the specific characteristic of cinchona bark. Starch grains are present in the parenchymatous tissues. Stone cells are rarely present in the structure. A few of the cork cells are lignified. Medullary rays are 2 to 3 cells wide.

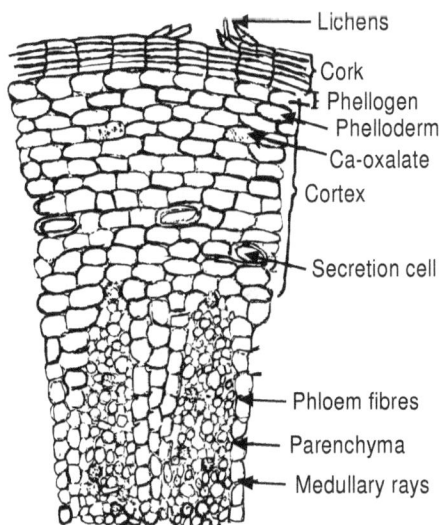

Fig. 2.18: T.S. of Cinchona Bark

Chemical Constituents

Cinchona bark contains about 25 alkaloids, which belong to quinoline group. The important alkaloids are quinine, quinidine, cinchonine and cinchonidine. The alkaloids of lesser importance are quinicine, cinchonicine hydroquinine, hydrocinchonidine and homocinchonidine. *C. succirubra* contains 5 - 7 per cent of total alkaloids, of which 30 per cent is quinine. *C. ledgeriana* yields from 6 - 10 per cent and, in some cases, upto 14 per cent of total alkaloids, with upto 75 per cent is quinine. *C. salisaya* has 6 - 8 per cent total alkaloids (about 50 per cent quinine).

Quinine and Quinidine are stereoisomers of each other. Quinidine is also obtained commercially from cuprea bark i.e. *Ramijia pendunculata* Fluckiger belonging to family Rubiaceae, or by isomerization of quinine.

Quinine and Quinidine form many salts, but medicinally their sulphates are more significant. Cinchonine and cinchonidine are also isomers of each other.

Apart from alkaloids, cinchona also contains quinic acid and cinchotannic acid. In the plant, the alkaloids are present as salts of these acids. Cinchotannic acid decomposes into insoluble cinchona red, due to its phlobatannin nature. Cinchona bark also contains a glycoside called quinovin, tannins and bitter essential oil.

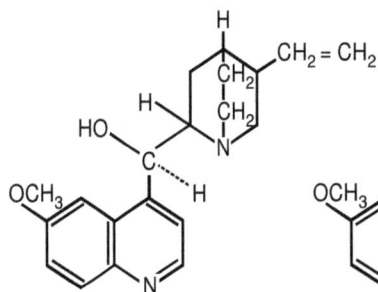

Quinine

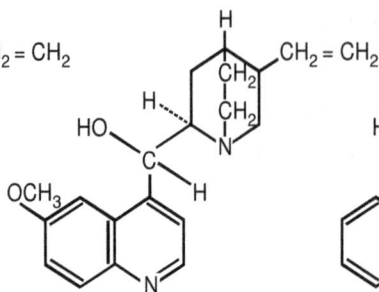

Qunidine

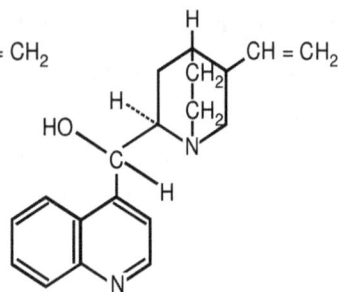

Cinchonine

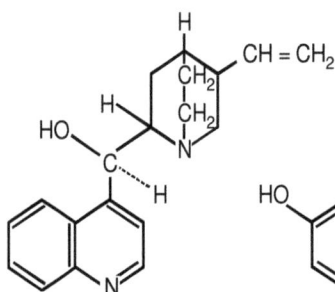

Cinchonidine

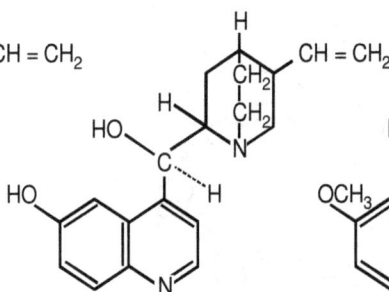

Cupreine

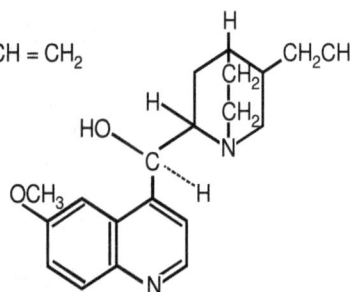

Hydroquinine

The alkaloid quinine occurs as bitter white crystals and it darkens when exposed to light and has fluorescent properties. It shows a strong blue fluorescence in ultra-violet light. This fluorescence is enhanced in presence of dilute sulphuric acid. Quinine forms salts with different acids. Quinine sulphate $(C_{20}H_{24}N_2O_2)_2$. H_2SO_4. $2H_2O$ is important from pharmaceutical point of view. It has very less solubility in water (1 in 810 parts of water), due to which, it is suitable for oral use.

Quinidine $(C_{20}H_{24}N_2O_2)$ is similar to quinine in its physical and chemical properties and has higher water solubility. The free base is soluble in water, ethyl alcohol, methyl alcohol and chloroform.

Chemical Tests

1. Heat the powdered drug in a dried test tube with little glacial acetic acid, purple vapours are produced at the upper part of test tube.

2. Thalleoquin test: The powdered drug gives emerald green colour with bromine water and dilute ammonia solution.

3. Quinidine solution gives a white precipitate with silver nitrate solution, which is soluble in nitric acid.

Standards

(1) Total ash   - not more than 4 per cent

(2) Foreign organic matter   - nor more than 2 per cent

The UV spectrophotometric method of estimation is carried out for quinine.

Uses

Cinchona bark is antimalarial in nature. The cinchona preparations like cinchona extract, compound cinchona tincture etc. are also employed as bitter stomachics and antipyretics. Quinine and its salts are used in the treatment of malaria. Quinine is a protoplasmic poison, especially for protozoa like *Plasmodium vivax, P. falciparum, P. malarie and P. fatal,* and hence, used as powerful antimalarial drug.

Recently the pharmacokinetic studies on quinine have shown that it can be better used in other forms. Infusion of quinine rather than intravenous injection eliminates the risk of sudden death. Secondly, quinine in microencapsulated form has been reported to give better bioavailability.

Quinine has also been found to be highly active *in vitro* against *Trypanosoma cruzi* epimastigotes.

Quinidine is primarily a cardiac depressant and used to prevent certain arrhythmias and tachycardia. Quinidine is valuable in prevention of atrial fibrillation.

Dose

1. Chinchona powder　　- 0.3 - 1 g
2. Quinine sulphate　　- 1 g daily for 2 days and then 600 mg daily for 5 days
3. Quinidine sulphate　- 0.2 - 0.4 g every two to four hours to a total dose of 3 g daily in atrial fibrillation.

Substitutes

Cuprea bark (*Remijia pedunculata*), a coppery red coloured drug, contains quinine, quinidine and other alkaloids which resemble to those from cinchona bark. The bark contains numerous stone cells. Along with cinchona alkaloids, it also contains cupreine. False cuprea bark (*R. purdiena*) contains an alkaloid called cusconidine, traces of cinchonine, cinchonamine, but no quinine.

CAMPTOTHECA

Synonyms

Cancer tree, Happy tree.

Biological Source

Camptotheca consist of the dried stem wood of *Camptotheca acuminata* Decne; *Camptotheca lowreyona* S.Y.Li. belonging to family *Nyssaceae* (Cornaceae).

Geographical Source

It is distributed in China and Tibet. It is indigenous to southern China. Camptothecin was discovered by National Institute of Health, U.S.A. during the antitumor screening programme for this plant.

Fig. 2.19: Camptotheca herb

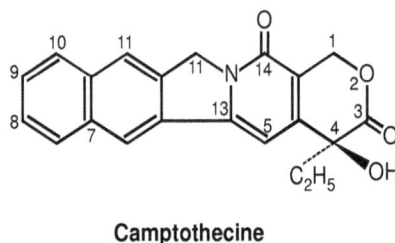

Camptothecine

Cultivation and Collection

It is a medium sized deciduous tree growing up to 10 metres and its plants can be raised by sowing the seeds or by means of vegetative propagation i.e. using the cuttings. Cultivation is done in autumn. Shading of whole seedlings increases the concentration of alkaloid in the leaves and lowers in the roots. Drought conditions increase the concentration of alkaloids in leaves. Fruits are collected late in autumn, while leaves, twigs, and bark is collected around the year. All plant parts are dried in the sunlight and then used.

Macroscopic Characters

Leaves are dark green in colour with reddish petiole. Leaves are entire, accuminate, ovate and lanceolate. 8-10 cm in length and 3-5 cm in width. Flowers are red coloured.

Taste: Bitter.

Chemical Constituents

Camptotheca plant contains 0.004 - 0.03 per cent of quinoline alkaloid camptothecin. Other minor constituents of the drug are Irinotecan, topotecan, 9-aminocamptothecin, 10-hydroxy camptothecin and 10-methoxy camptothecin. All plant parts leaves, bark, fruits, and twigs also contain camptothecin, young leaves have highest concentration.

Camptothecin has yellow needle shaped crystals. It is a very weak basic alkaloid and does not form stable salts with mineral acids. It does not respond Dragendorff's and Mayer's reagent test. The other minor constituents are 10-hydroxycamptothecin and 10-methoxycamptothecin.

Uses

Camptothecin is prototype DNA topoisomerase I inhibitor. It has shown a broad spectrum antitumour activity in animal tests. Its sodium salt shows pronounced antileukemic activities. Preliminary and Phase II clinical studies of sodium salt for gastrointestinal cancer have given promising results, but show extremely high toxicity in both animals and human beings.

Camptothecin inhibits the replication of DNA viruses such as herpes virus, adenovirus and vaccinia virus, but shows no effect on RNA virus like poliovirus.

Camptothecin and 10-hydroxycamptothecin are used in China, clinically, for treatment of leukemia and liver cancer. Their toxicity is less than sodium salt of camptothecin.

[4] ISOQUINOLINE ALKALOIDAL DRUGS

OPIUM

Synonym

Raw opium

Biological Source

It is the dried latex obtained by incision from the unripe capsules of *Papaver somniferum* Linn., dried or partly dried by heat or spontaneous evaporation, and worked into somewhat irregularly shaped masses (natural opium) or moulded into masses of more uniform size and shape (manipulated opium). Poppy plant belongs to family Papaveraceae. It contains not less than 10 per cent of morphine, and not less than 2.0 per cent of codeine, both calculated as anhydrous morphine.

Geographical Source

India, Pakistan, Afghanistan, Turkey, Russia, China, and Iran.

History

Opium has been known to mankind since centuries due to its narcotic properties. It was first cultivated in Mediterranean regions and probably brought by Alexander in 327 B.C. to India. It is known that Dioscorides and Theophrastus were aware of the medicinal properties of opium. The earliest written record about opium is revealed from *Historia plantarum* (some where in 300 B.C.) and *De Materia Medica* (78 A.D.). Narcotine was the first alkaloid reported both from opium and among alkaloidal series, to be isolated in 1803 by Derosne. Segnin isolated morphine in 1804. Magendi and Bally first introduced it in medical practice in 1818. Gulland and Robinson elucidated the structure of morphine in 1923. In 1833, Robiquet isolated codeine from opium, and in 1881, Grimaux reported that codeine is o-methyl derivative of morphine. Merck company isolated papaverine in 1848.

Cultivation, Collection and Preparation

Being a potent narcotic drug, the cultivation and other aspects of opium are governed by respective governments in different countries, including India. In India, all the activities about opium and its derivatives are controlled under Narcotic Drugs and Psychotropic Substances Act, 1985.

The genus *Papaver* has 50 different species, of which six species are found in India, viz. *P. somniferum* (Opium poppy), *P. nudicaule* (Iceland poppy), *P. rhoeas* (corn poppy), *P. orientale*, *P. argemone*, and *P. dubium*.

Poppy is an erect plant attaining 60 - 120 cm height. It is rarely branched. The leaves are linear, oblong or ovate oblong and have a dentate or serrate margin. It bears bluish white, purple or violet coloured large flowers. Accordingly, the varieties *P. somniferum* var. *glabrum*, *P. somniferum* var.

album, P. somniferum var. nigrum are described. The second variety is cultivated in India. Indian opium is considered as the only legal source of opium to many countries including United States of America and Britain.

In India, about 54 thousand hectares of land is under opium poppy cultivation. It is under government control, and cultivation of poppy is restricted to Madhya Pradesh, Rajasthan and Uttar Pradesh.

The weather conditions affect, up to a large extent, the yield of opium. Although, temperate climate is the natural requirement of opium poppy, it can be grown with success under subtropical climate in winter season, as there is a favourable effect on yield by cold weather. But, extreme cold conditions, including frost, adversely affect the plant and ultimately yield of opium. In short, the best climatic conditions for opium poppy are cool weather without freezing temperature and cloudiness, and sufficient sunshine.

Opium poppy is grown from November to March. Propagation is done by sowing the seeds, for which 3 - 4 kg of seeds per hectare are necessary. The seeds admixed with about 3 - 4 parts of sand are sown. Opium poppy requires highly fertile, well drained loamy soil with fine sand. The soil should contain organic matter, nitrogen and should have a pH around 7. The distance between two plants maintained is usually 25 cm and the plant reaches maximum height of one metre. Periodically, the thinning of plants is done to get uniform growth and better development. The plants are kept totally free from weeds with the use of suitable weedicides. The plant should be protected from various insect pests like cut worms, leaf minor and poppy borer. The use of manures and fertilizers markedly improve the quality and yield of opium poppy. Especially, nitrogen and phosphorus have remarkable effects on growth of plant.

After sowing, within 3 - 4 months, the plant bears flowers, which are converted to capsules within few days and attain maturity after 15 - 20 days. During the maturity period, the capsule exudes maximum latex which shows a colour change from dark green to light green. Such capsules (Fig. 2.16) are incised vertically in the afternoon with the help of specific needle like apparatus called 'nushtur'. It penetrates maximum up to 2 mm into the capsule. Because of incisions, latex exudes out and thickens due to cold weather in night which is eventually scrapped and collected next morning by an iron scoop called *Charpala*. The incising process is repeated for about 4 times on the same capsule with 2 days interval. The incisions must remain superficial, so as to maintain the external exudation of latex. The latex is collected in plastic containers. Then, capsules are collected and dried in open areas and further the seeds are separated by beating. The average yield of opium is about 25-26 kg per hectare and for seeds, it is from 4-5 quintals per hectare. Opium is exported traditionally from India. The exports for 95-96 and 96-97 were ₹ 2365.5 lacs and 4102 lacs respectively.

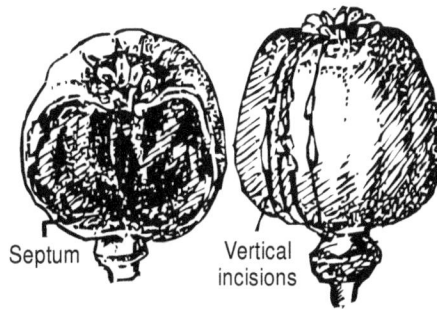

Fig. 2.20: Poppy Capsules

The opium collected by this way is either exported or some of the part is further processed at Government opium factory at Ghazipur. A generalised process is outlined to cover the industrial method for extraction of alkaloids of opium.

Macroscopic Characters

Odour : Strong characteristic

Taste : bitter

1. Indian opium: Dark brown in colour. It is found in the form of cubical pieces weighing about 900 g for marketing purposes. It is enclosed in tissue paper and is brittle and plastic in nature. Internally, it is homogenous. Depending upon the requirement, the powdered form is available in the pack of 5 to 10 kg.

2. Persian opium: Dark brown in colour, found in the form of brick shaped masses, weighing 450 g. It is hygroscopic in nature, granular or nearly smooth with brittle fracture.

3. Natural Turkish or European opium: Brown or dark brown in colour. It is found in conical or rounded and somewhat flattened masses, weighing 250 to 1000 g. On keeping, it becomes hard and brittle. It is covered with poppy leaves.

4. Manipulated Turkish opium: It is chocolate brown or dark brown internally and covered with broken poppy leaves externally. The masses of this type are oval and flattened on upper and lower surface weighing about 2000 g. It is somewhat plastic or even brittle.

5. Manipulated European opium: It is dark brown in colour internally and covered with broken leaves. It is found in the form of elongated masses with rounded ends weighing 150 to 500 g. It is firm, plastic and with brittle fracture.

Chemical Constituents

The latex contains mainly the alkaloids derived from amino acids phenylalanine and tyrosine. Chemically, they are placed under benzylisoquinoline and phenanthrene types.

Narcotine (also called noscapine), narceine and papaverine belong to the former, while morphine, codeine and thebaine represent latter category.

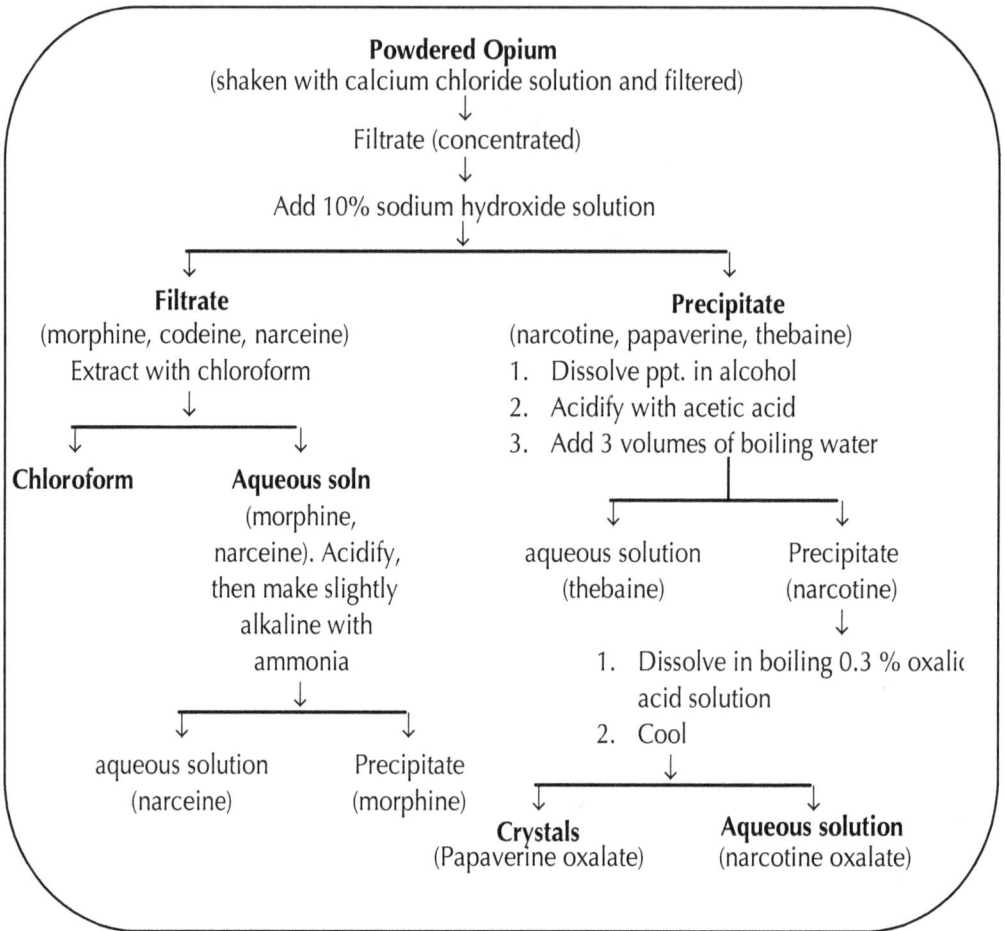

Powdered Opium
(shaken with calcium chloride solution and filtered)
↓
Filtrate (concentrated)
↓
Add 10% sodium hydroxide solution
↓

Filtrate
(morphine, codeine, narceine)
Extract with chloroform
↓

Chloroform　　　**Aqueous soln**
(morphine,
narceine). Acidify,
then make slightly
alkaline with
ammonia
↓

aqueous solution　　　Precipitate
(narceine)　　　(morphine)

Precipitate
(narcotine, papaverine, thebaine)
1. Dissolve ppt. in alcohol
2. Acidify with acetic acid
3. Add 3 volumes of boiling water

aqueous solution　　　Precipitate
(thebaine)　　　(narcotine)
↓
1. Dissolve in boiling 0.3 % oxalic
acid solution
2. Cool
↓

Crystals　　　**Aqueous solution**
(Papaverine oxalate)　　　(narcotine oxalate)

Fruits of poppy contain numerous off white coloured and minute seeds. These seeds contain 30-35 per cent drying fixed oil. Which is used commercially in oil paint industry, which is colourless, tasteless and transparent.

OPIUM ALKALOIDS

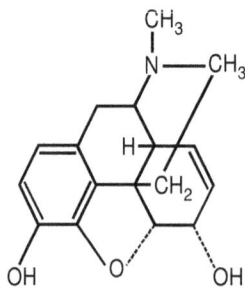

Morphine

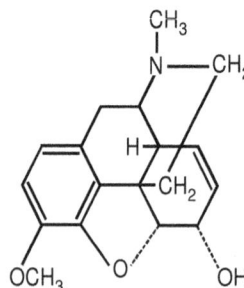

Codeine

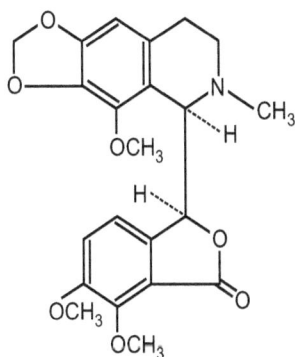

Narcotine

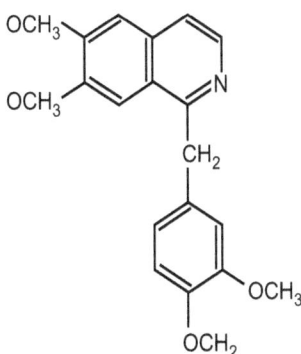

Papaverine

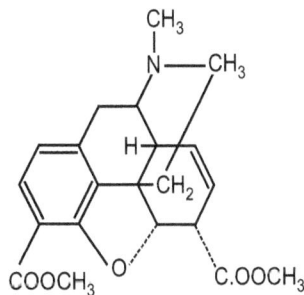

Heroin

Morphine is monoacidic, laevorotatory phenolic alkaloid and also contains an alcoholic hydroxyl group at C (6) position. Due to presence of phenolic hydroxyl group, it is soluble in alkali hydroxides, except ammonium hydroxide. Morphine is very less soluble in different solvents like ether (1 in 600), chloroform (1 in 1200), alcohol (1 in 200) and water (1 - 3000). Diacetyl derivative of morphine is heroin.

Codeine (methyl morphine) is a strong monoacidic base and laevorotatory. It is soluble in water and organic solvents.

Papaverine is a weak monoacidic base and inactive optically. It is slightly soluble in organic solvents, but insoluble in water.

The other important benzylisoquinoline alkaloid narcotine is also a weak monoacidic base and is laevorotatory, while its salts are dextrorotatory. Narcotine is soluble in acetone, benzene, chloroform, but insoluble in water, alcohol and ether.

The opium alkaloids are present as salts of meconic acid.

Protopine and hydrocotarnine are the minor alkaloids of opium. Opium also contains sugar, wax, mucilage and salts of calcium, potassium and magnesium. Opium does not contain tannins, starch and calcium oxalate.

Chemical Tests

The general test to detect opium is by testing presence of meconic acid. The alkaloids are present as the salts of meconic acid.

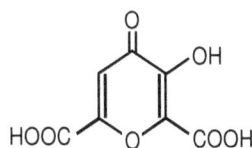

Meconic acid

(1) Opium is dissolved in water and to the filtrate, ferric chloride solution is added by which deep reddish purple colour is obtained, which persists even on addition of hydrochloric acid.

(2) Morphine when sprinkled on nitric acid gives orange red colour. Codeine does not respond to this test.

(3) The treatment of morphine solution with potassium ferricyanide and ferric chloride solutions gives bluish green colour. Codeine does not respond to this test.

(4) Papaverine solution in hydrochloric acid gives a lemon yellow colour with potassium ferricyanide solution.

Uses

Opium belongs to the category of hypnotic sedative and analgesic in which the action is mainly due to morphine. Morphine is a potent analgesic. Due to its central narcotic effects, it causes addiction. Hence, it is given only in severe pains and in those cases, when patient does not show response to other analgesics. Morphine has a biphasic action on central nervous system. It sedates the cerebrum and has a mixture of stimulation and sedation on the medulla. In the medulla, it sedates the respiratory centre, emetic centre and the cough reflex. It also stimulates chemoreceptor trigger zone in the medulla, which leads to nausea and vomitting and is considered as a side effect. Morphine also produces respiratory depression and constipation.

Codeine relieves local irritation in the bronchial tract and as an antitussive used in various cough medicines. It has mild analgesic effects, which are potent than aspirin, but only one tenth activity of that of morphine. Papaverine has relaxant effects on smooth muscles of the intestinal and bronchial tract and the blood vessels. Narcotine has a specific depressant action on cough reflex and used in the preparation of cough linctuses.

Opium alkaloids are semisynthesized like other medicinal agents. Diacetyl morphine (heroin) has more narcotic, analgesic property than morphine. By losing one molecule of water, morphine gives apomorphine which is emetic and used subcutaneously to treat poisoning cases. Hydromorphone is formed by replacing one of the hydroxyl groups and also removal of adjacent double bond. It is also a potent narcotic analgesic, but habit forming tendencies are less.

The synthetic morphine like compounds are called 'opioids', which are non habit forming, but possess the medicinal activity of morphine.

Dose

(1) Morphine Sulphate	:	10 mg, 6 times a day parenterally.
(2) Codeine sulphate/phosphate	:	10 - 20 mg every 4 - 6 hours, orally.
(3) Narcotine (noscapine)	:	15 mg, 4 times a day, orally.
(4) Papaverine hydrochloride	:	150 mg orally and 30 mg parenterally.

Commercial Varieties of Opium

(1) Indian opium: It is dark brown in colour and found in the form of cubical pieces weighing 900 g. It is brittle and plastic in nature. The powdered form is available as 5 - 10 kg packs. It contains 10 per cent anhydrous morphine.

(2) Persian opium: It is dark brown in colour and available as brick shaped masses of 450 g. It is hygroscopic, granular or smooth.

(3) Turkish opium: It is commonly called as druggists opium or soft opium. It is brown or dark brown in colour and available as conical rounded or flattened masses.

(4) Chinese opium: It comes in market in the form of flat globular cakes and contains 4 - 11 per cent morphine.

Different Forms of Opium

(1) **Powdered opium:**		It contains 10 per cent anhydrous morphine with lactose, caramel and powdered cocoa husks.
(2) **Opium concentratum:**		It contains different alkaloid hydrochlorides of opium in following proportions:
Anhydrous morphine	-	47.5 - 52.5 per cent
Codeine	-	2.5 - 5 per cent
Narcotine	-	16 - 22 per cent
Papaverine	-	2.5 - 7 per cent

(3) **Camphorated opium tincture**: It contains alcoholic solution of opium, benzoic acid, camphor, anise oil and the formulation is prepared in alcohol. It is used in treatment of diarrhoea as antiperistaltic.

Storage

Opium is preserved in a well closed container to prevent loss of morphine.

Adulteration

Since the production of opium is under government control, it is not found to be adulterated. The adulterated forms show presence of opium capsules in powdered form, gum and sugary fruits.

Allied Plants

The various other species of poppy, which do not contain morphine are *Papaver argemone, P. dubium, P. orientate, P. bracteatum, P. strigosum, P. intermedia, P. paeoniflorum*, hybrid of *P. somniferum* and *P. orientate, P. pseudo orientale*, and plants from genera *Argemone* and *Eschscholzia* (both belonging to family Papaveraceae).

Among all these species, *P. bracteatum* has scored more importance, as it does not contain morphine, which causes addiction. The amount of total alkaloids and consequent percentage of thebaine is also very high. Because of such morphine free contents, this species is more significant as a potential new source of opiates.

IPECACUANHA

Synonym

Ipecac

Biological Source

It consists of the dried roots, or the rhizomes and roots of *Cephaelis ipecacuanha* (Brot.) A. Rich. or of *Cephaelis acuminata* Karsten, both belonging to family Rubiaceae. It should contain not less than 2 per cent of the total alkaloids, in which at least 50 per cent should be emetine.

Geographical Source

Cephaelis ipecacuanha is called Rio or Brazilian ipecac, which is obtained from Brazil, India, Myanmar, and Malaysia. *C. acuminata* is called Panama or Cartagena ipecac, which is procured from Columbia, Panama, Nicaragua and India.

History

Ipecacuanha means the small wayside plant with vomiting effects. Even before it was introduced in Europe as a medicine, ipecac was known in Brazil and used as an antidysenteric drug. Helvetius, a Dutch physician, launched use of this drug in Europe in 1688 under the name Brazilian root. In 1817, Pelletier and Magnedi first isolated emetine in crude form and later in 1894, Paul and Cownley separated emetine in pure form. Pyman succeeded in isolating two more alkaloids, viz. emetamine and o–methyl psychotrine in 1917.

Cultivation, Collection and Preparation

The commercial cultivation of Rio ipecac (also called Brazilian or Matto Grosso ipecac) in India is discussed here as large areas from West Bengal are under the cultivation of Rio ipecac. The drug from W. Bengal is also called as Johore ipecac. Better results have been obtained by cultivating ipecac at the lower foot hills of Eastern Himalayas. But the cultivation needs special attention and precautions.

The propagation is done by sowing the seeds in mid January to mid February. The germination is improved by treatment of seeds with lime water or hydrogen peroxide. The two months old seedlings are transplanted at a spacing of 10 × 10 cm. It favourably grows in the temperature range of 23 - 38°C, with a rainfall of 300 cm. The humid atmosphere helps in the growth of plant. The nitrogenous fertilizers have significant effect in increasing the quantity of emetine. The percentage of all alkaloids is maximum in third year and hence, harvesting of roots is done after three years of vegetative growth.

Macroscopic characters (Fig. 2.21)

1. Brazilian ipecacuanha

(a) Roots

Colour - Dark brick red to dark brown

Odour - Faint

Taste - Bitter

Size - Up to 150 mm in length and 6 mm in thickness

Shape - Roots are found in tortuous pieces.

Fig. 2.21: Ipecacuanha herb & root

Extra Features

They are closely annulated externally, ridges rounded and completely encircling roots. Fracture is short in the bark and splintery in the wood. Pith is absent.

(b) Rhizomes

Colour - Brick red to dark brown.

Size - About 2 mm in diameter and short, attached to the roots

Shape - Cylindrical.

Extra Features

They are wrinkled longitudinally and show the presence of prominent pith.

2. Panama ipecacuanha

Colour   -   Greyish-brown to reddish-brown

Odour and taste   -   Same as in Brazilian variety

Size   -   Characterized by large size upto 9 mm in thickness.

Shape   -   Cylindrical

Extra Features

They are characterised by the absence of annulations and the presence of transverse ridges at an interval of 1 to 3 mm. They partially encircle the roots.

Microscopic Characters (Fig. 2.22)

Roots: Transverse section of root shows the presence of cork layer with brown contents, which is followed by phelloderm composed of thin walled parenchyma. It is full of starch grains and acicular crystals of calcium oxalate. Xylem consists of tracheids and small vessels. Secondary medullary rays with starch grains are also present. Size of the starch grains is up to 15 microns.

Rhizomes: Pericycle is with thick walled sclereids, protoxylem and spiral vessels. Columbian variety differs only in one aspect i.e. the starch grains are larger in size and up to 22 microns.

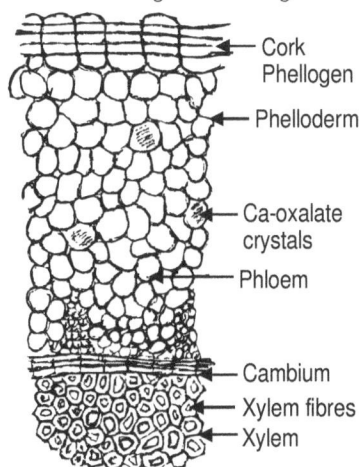

Fig. 2.22: T. S. of Ipecacuanha Root

Chemical Constituents

Ipecac contains isoquinoline alkaloids which belong to phenolic and non phenolic groups. The total alkaloids in Rio-ipecac are upto 2 per cent, and in Panama ipecac, about 2.2 per cent. The main alkaloids are emetine, cephaeline, psychotrine, o-methyl psychotrine and emetamine. The proportion of emetine and cephaeline in different varieties is 4 : 1 (Rio-ipecac), 1 : 1 (Panama/ cartagena), 2.5 : 1 (Johore), alongwith minor bases like psychotrine, emetamine and o-methyl psychotrine.

Cephaeline is converted into emetine by methylation of phenolic C (6) hydroxyl group. Medicinally, emetine is most important. Non phenolic alkaloidal group includes emetine and o-methyl psychotrine, while phenolic alkaloidal group includes cephaeline and psychotrine. Ipecac also contains ipecacuanhic acid, glycoside ipecacuanhin, starch and calcium oxalate.

Chemical Tests

(1) To about 2.5 g powdered drug, add 20 ml hydrochloric acid and 5 ml water. Shake it well and filter. To the filtrate, add 0.5 g potassium chlorate. The presence of yellow colour gradually changing to red, after standing, is due to emetine.

(2) The addition of sulphuric acid and sodium molybdate (Frohde's reagent) to small quantity of emetine gives bright green colour.

Standards

(1) Total ash   - not more than 5 per cent
(2) Acid-insoluble ash   - not more than 2 per cent
(3) Foreign organic matter   - not more than 1 per cent

Emetine $R_1 = CH_3$
Cephaeline $R_1 = OH$

O-methyl psychotrine $R_2 = CH_3$
Psychotrine $R_2 = H$

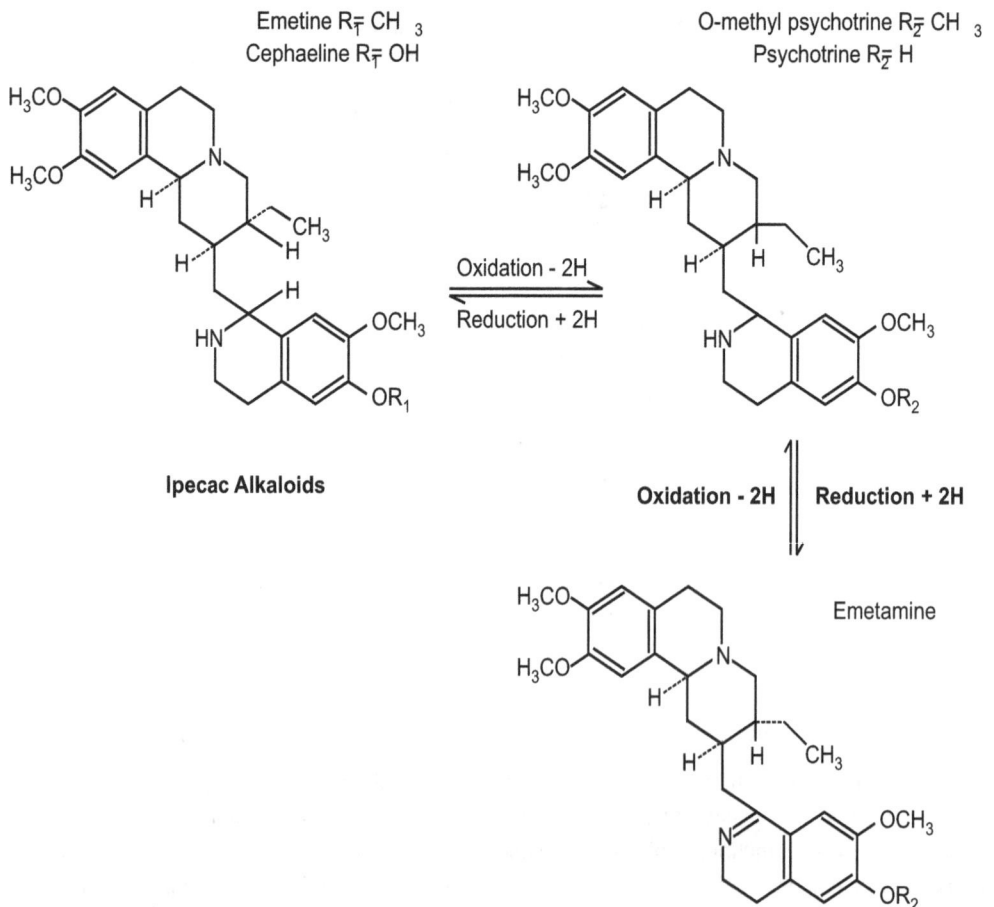

Oxidation - 2H
Reduction + 2H

Ipecac Alkaloids

Oxidation - 2H   Reduction + 2H

Emetamine

Uses

Ipecacuanha is expectorant in small doses and emetic in higher doses. Cephaeline has more emetic and less expectorant action as compared to emetine.

Emetine hydrochloride is used as antiprotozoal, as it is highly toxic to amoeba i.e. *Entamoeba histolytica* even in very low concentrations like 1 in 6 millions. Hence, it is used by administering parenterally, in treatment of amoebic dysentery.

Ipecacuanha is used for isolation of emetine and cephaeline. It is also reported that emetine has anti-tumour properties.

Dose

Emetine hydrochloride: 1 mg per kg body weight, subcutaneously or intramuscularly, but should not exceed 60 mg and maximum for 5 days.

Allied Plants

Various genera belonging to family Rubiaceae contain emetine. Some of them are *Alangium, Hillia, Manettia Psychotria, Borreria, Remijia* and *Ferdinandusa.*

[5] INDOLE ALKALOIDAL DRUGS

Most of the indole alkaloids are biosynthesized in the plants from amino acid tryptophan. It is considered as one of the most important group of alkaloids, as they yield the drugs with very useful therapeutic effects. The indole alkaloids normally contain two nitrogens, out of which one is present as indolic nitrogen and the other one is present in the position created by removal of two carbons from the p-position of the indole ring.

The crude drugs containing indole nucleus are discussed here.

ERGOT

Synonyms

Ergot of Rye, Ergota.

Biological Source

Ergot is the dried sclerotium of a fungus, *Claviceps purpurea* Tulasne (Clavicipitaceae or Hypocraceae) developed in ovary of rye plant, *Secale cereale* Linne (Graminae). It contains not less than 0.19 per cent of the total alkaloids of ergot, calculated as ergotoxine, of which not less than 15 per cent consists of water soluble alkaloids of ergot, calculated as ergometrine.

Geographical Source

Switzerland, Yugoslavia, Hungary and Czechoslovakia.

History

The name of this drug is originated from a French word 'Argot,' which means fur and indicates the shape and attachment of the sclerotia to the infected rye spikes, like the fur which is attached to the body of the birds. Even in old days, ergot fungus was known to be a pathogen, infecting the rye fields in European countries and Russia. It is known that the toxic effects were observed owing to contamination of ergot with rye grains. The toxic symptoms were gangrene in the extremities and convulsions. In middle ages, such symptoms were reported and called as St. Antony's fire. After knowing the cause, it was called as ergotism which had severely occured in sixteenth century in Germany. Further, it was discovered that ergot has specific uses in obstetrics and came into wide use from nineteenth century onwards. In 1836, it was introduced in London Pharmacopoeia. The life history of fungus was studied and the name *Claviceps purpurea* was first coined by Tulasne in 1853.

Collection and Preparation of Ergot

Presently, ergot is produced by natural way i.e. cultivation of rye plants and subsequently infecting with this fungus, as well as, by artificial way i.e. saprophytic production.

For the natural way of production, rye plant is host and ergot is a parasite. It is known that more than 600 plants from different families of wild and cultivated grasses act as hosts for ergot fungus as a parasite or pathogen. The various other known species of this fungus are *C. microcephala*, *C. nigricans* and *C. paspali*, which can produce ergot. Among all the hosts, rye is the better host for the large scale production of ergot by way of quality and quantity.

Among the various stages of development of this fungus, sclerotial stage or a dormant stage contains the maximum amount of drug. For a systematic study, it is necessary to know the other developmental stages of fungus or more precisely the life history of ergot (*Fig. 2.23*)

Life Cycle of Ergot (Fig. 2.23)

Fig. 2.23: Life Cycle of Ergot

The ovary of the rye plant at its base, gets infected by ascospores of the fungus in spring or summer season. The spread of ascospores to ovaries is influenced by wind and insects. After infecting, the ascospore germinate in the favourable conditions, like moisture and damp climate. The germination of ascospores leads to formation of hyphal strands which go on invading the wall of ovary with the help of an enzyme. By this way, the hyphae form a soft, white mass of tissue over the surface of the ovary which is called as mycelium. The mycelium secrets a viscous and sugary fluid called honey-dew. At the same time, the hyphal strands produce asexual spores called conidiospores, which remain in a suspended form in honey-dew. Due to the sugary fluid i.e. honey-dew, the insects and ants are attracted which further help in the spread of the fungus to other host plants. This developmental stage is the sexual stage and called as **Sphacelial stage**.

The hyphae further invade into the deeper parts of ovary and slowly replace the entire tissue of ovary by a compact tissue called pseudoparenchyma which is hard and dark purple. It is called as **Sclerotium stage** and is considered as resting or dormant stage of the fungus and contains maximum amount of ergot alkaloids. If this sclerotium is left uncollected, it eventually falls on the ground and in the favourable season, i.e. spring gives out 'stromata' which are in the elongated form. Each stromatum has a globular head and a stalk. The head portion contains a large number of perithecia and every perithecium is like a flask shaped structure which contains a number of sacs, each sac containing the ascospores which are thread like in appearance. Ascospores are the sexual spores capable of inducing fresh life cycle of fungus by infecting the ovary of rye plant.

Selection of a correct strain of fungus (*Claviceps purpurea*), appropriate containers for preparing large scale ergot inoculum and an ideal nutrient medium are important requirements for commercial production of ergot. The various chemical races of fungus can produce only specific ergot alkaloids like ergotamine, ergometrine and ergotoxin in appreciable quantities from their sclerotia. The ascospores of this species with the specific chemical race are germinated on nutritive medium and by this way large bulk of conidiospores are formed. The suspension of this strain of fungus is sprayed on rye plants in large cultivated areas.

Apart from field cultivation, other method which is much practised is saprophytic production of ergot. This process was initiated in Japan by Prof. Abe. Saprophytic production is convenient in many ways as it eliminates the variation in yield due to weather conditions and production can be achieved throughout the year. For this method, various strains of ergot are used depending on the type of ergot alkaloid to be obtained. *Claviceps paspali* gives clavines and simple lysergic acid derivatives.

It is much easier to manufacture clavines and simple lysergic acid derivatives and then convert them to different peptide alkaloids, i.e. ergot alkaloids. For nutrition of cultures of fungus, specific nutrients are used and fermentation is carried out in temperature range of 20°C - 30°C and in a pH of 4.6 - 6.3. The fermentation process for these submerged cultures in shaking flasks or fermenters takes from 7 - 21 days. The isolation, separation and purification of simple lysergic acid derivatives or synthesized alkaloids is done by usual ways applied for other alkaloids. The lysergic acid derivatives are converted to lysergic acid and further partly synthesized into ergometrine and other peptide alkaloids.

The saprophytic production is much practised now-a-days, because mycelial dry weight gives even more than 20 per cent of alkaloids, while natural sclerotia contain less than 1 per cent of alkaloids. The process of fermentation is properly regulated or controlled for optimum bioproduction of useful metabolites.

Macroscopic Characters (Fig. 2.24)

Colour - Externally, it is dark violet to black. Internally, it is whitish or pinkish white.

Odour - Disagreeable and faint.

Taste - Unpleasant.

Size - The sclerotia are 1 - 3 cm in length and 1 - 5 mm in width.

Shape - Sclerotia are fusiform, triangular and usually tapering on both the ends.

Fracture - It is brittle with short fracture.

Fig. 2.24: Sclerotia of Ergot

Extra Features

Longitudinal furrows and transverse cracks are present on each surface. Sclerotia are highly susceptible for fungal growth.

Microscopic Characters (Fig. 2.25)

The outermost layer of the sclerotium is made up of few thin, flattened, polygonal cells of purple to dark brown colour, while inner part is made up of dense pseudo parenchymatous cells composed of chitin. The mycelial cells (central region) are round or oval, thick and with high refractive walls. They also contain cells with fixed oil. Sclerotium does not contain starch, calcium oxalate or any of the lignified tissue.

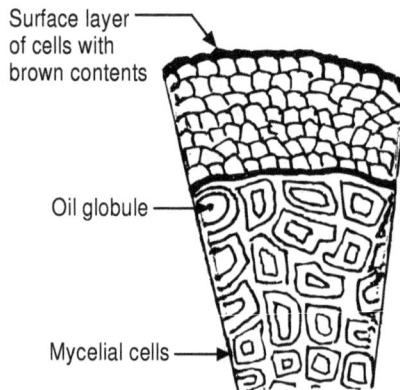

Surface layer of cells with brown contents

Oil globule

Mycelial cells

Fig. 2.25: T.S. of Sclerotium of Ergot

Chemical Constituents

Ergot contains large number of potent indole alkaloids (0.1 - 0.25 per cent), which are derivatives of lysergic acid. Lysergic acid is present in its peptide derivative form and hence the alkaloids are also called as peptide alkaloids. The six pairs of alkaloids are broadly grouped into water soluble and water insoluble categories. Each pair contains laevo-form which is medicinally active, while dextro form is inert in action. The water soluble pair contains (–) ergometrine and its dextro part as ergometrinine. The water insoluble group is further divided into Ergotamine and ergotoxine group.

Table 2.4: Ergot alkaloids

(–) Laevorotatory alkaloids		(+) Dextrorotatory alkaloids
Ergometrine	Water-Soluble	Ergometrinine
Ergotamine		Ergotaminine
Ergosine		Ergosinine
Ergocristine	Water insoluble	Ergocristinine
Ergocryptine		Ergocryptinine
Ergocornine		Ergocorninine

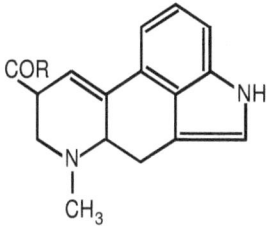   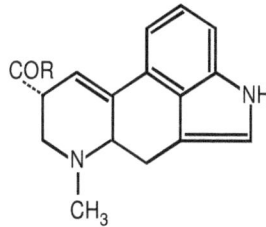

R = – OH	Lysergic acid	Isolysergic acid
R = –NH$_2$	Lysergic acid amide	Isolysergic acid amide
	(Ergine)	**(Erginine)**

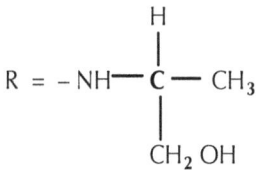

R = – NH—C—CH$_3$ (with H above C and CH$_2$OH below C)   Ergometrine   Ergometrinine

R = – N (C$_2$H$_5$)$_2$ Lysergic acid diethylamide (LSD)

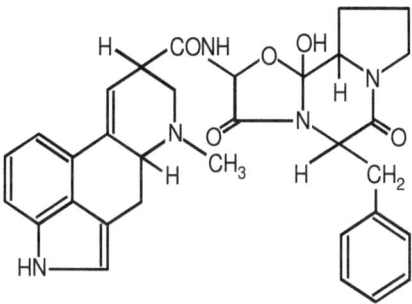

Ergotamine

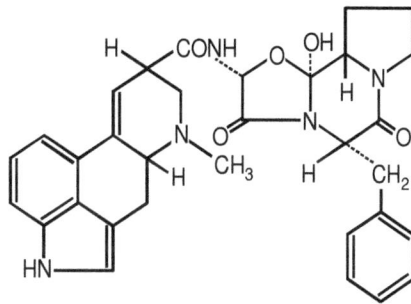

Ergocristine

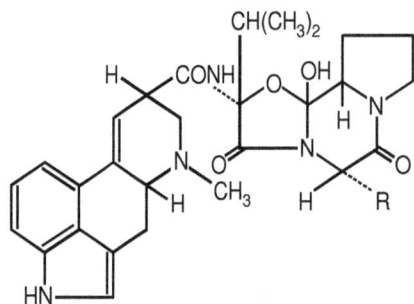

Ergocryptine

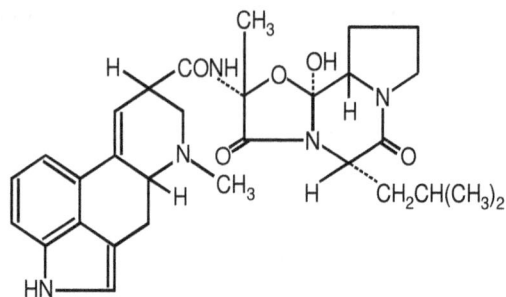

Ergosine

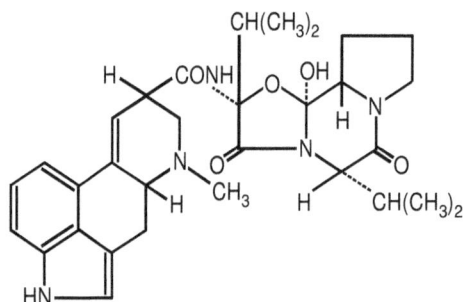

Ergocornine

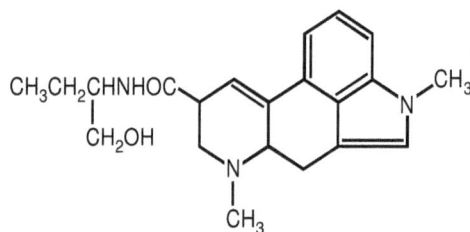

Methysergide

α-Ergocryptine	R = CH₂CH(CH₃)₂
β-Ergocryptine	R = CH(CH₃)CH₂CH₃

α-Ergocryptine   R = $CH_2CH(CH_3)_2$
β-Ergocryptine   R = $CH(CH_3)CH_2CH_3$

(Derivative of Lysergic acid used as migraine prophylactic)

Besides the alkaloids, ergot also contains pigments, ergosterol and fungisterol, histamine, tyramine, amino acids, acetyl choline, chitin, up to 30 per cent fixed oil and 8 per cent moisture.

Chemical Tests

1. Ergot powder gives a blue colour with p-dimethylaminobenzaldehyde (Van-Urk's reagent).

2. Ergot is treated with solvent ether and sulphuric acid and the filtrate obtained shows red violet colour in its aqueous layer, when treated with saturated solution of sodium bicarbonate.

3. Ergometrine gives a blue fluorescence in water.

4. Ergotamine responds to a specific test. Little quantity of ergotamine is dissolved in glacial acetic acid and ethyl acetate. A small portion of this is treated with sulphuric acid and shaken well by which blue colour with red tinge appears. By addition of ferric chloride, blue colour deepens, while red tinge becomes faint.

Standardisation

Ergot and its alkaloids are analysed by spectrocolorimetric method and bio assay is carried out for oxytocic activity.

Uses

Ergot and its alkaloids have many different uses. Now-a-days, ergot is not used as a whole, but the isolated alkaloids are used in therapeutics. Ergot and ergometrine maleate (in the United States, ergometrine is called as ergonovine) are used as oxytocic and sometimes used to enhance the labour pains in delivery cases and also to prevent the post partum haemorrhage. Ergotamine tartarate is used as a specific analgesic in treatment of migraine. It is given along with caffeine. Ergotoxine methanesulphonates (mesylates) are used in geriatric patients. Lysergic acid diethylamide (LSD) is a semisynthetic derivative, and possesses psychotomimetic action and used in psychiatry, but owing to its abuse, its use is controlled under Narcotic Drugs and Psychotropic Substances Act, 1985.

As ergometrine and methyl ergometrine are important drugs in obstetrics, their pharmacology is discussed here in brief. Both of them are structurally similar ergot alkaloid derivatives that share similar mechanism of action and activities. Both of them have the capacity to directly stimulate contractions of uterine and vascular smooth muscles by interacting with tryptaminergic, dopaminergic and alpha-adrenergic receptors. Small doses produce uterine contractions with increased force and frequency and with normal resting muscle tone. Intermediate doses cause more forceful and prolonged contractions with an elevated resting muscle tone, while large doses cause sustained contractions and tetany. Small doses of these drugs are used after delivery to control bleeding and maintain uterine firmness. Methyl ergometrine is generally preferred, because it causes less hypertension.

Dose

1. Ergometrine maleate and methyl ergometrine maleate, oral 200 – 400 µg, 2 - 4 times a day, i.m./i.v. → 200 µg every 6-8 hours.

2. Ergotamine tartarate → 1 - 2 mg sublingual; 250 - 500 µg intramuscular/subcutaneous.

3. Ergotoxine methanesulphonates → 0.5 mg sublingual, 4 - 6 times a day

Prepared Ergot

The powdered and immediately defatted ergot is called as prepared ergot. It is required to contain 0.19 per cent of total ergot alkaloids, calculated as ergotoxine of which 15 per cent should be ergometrine. Its dose is 0.15 - 0.5 g by oral route.

Storage

Ergot should be dried thoroughly and kept in entire form in cool place. It should be stored in well closed containers. Ergot alkaloids are very sensitive to moisture and hence thorough drying of ergot is necessary. The broken sclerotia are very susceptible to the fungal growth and hence broken pieces should not be stored. Ergot alkaloids are sensitive to light and temperature. Hence, the drug is stored at low temperature in cool place away from light. If powdered ergot is required to be stored, it should be defatted first and then stored or, otherwise, decomposition of active constituents takes place.

RAUWOLFIA

Synonyms

Rauwolfia root, Serpentina root, Chhotachand, Serpgandha.

Biological Source

Rauwolfia consists of dried roots of the plant known as *Rauwolfia serpentina* Benth, belonging to family Apocynaceae. Serpgandha contains not less than 0.15 per cent of reserpine and ajmalcine, calculated on dried basis.

Geographical Source

Several species of *Rauwolfia* are found distributed in the tropical regions of Asia, America and Africa. Commercially, it is produced in India, Sri Lanka, Myanmar, Thailand and America. In India, it is cultivated in Uttar Pradesh, Bihar, Orissa, Tamil Nadu, West Bengal, Karnataka, Maharashtra, and Gujarat.

History

This drug is known to Indian System of Medicine since last many centuries. Because of snake like shape of the drug, it has been known as 'Sarpagandha'. It has found its place as an important drug in treatment of insanity and snake bite since traditional times. But the drug came into limelight only after the isolation of reserpine, its most significant alkaloid, in 1952 by Mueller. Since then a large interest has been generated regarding the activity of this drug.

Cultivation and Collection

Under wide range of climatic conditions, rauwolfia grows luxuriantly. However, it flourishes in hot humid condition and grows satisfactorily in shade. In wild state, it grows in variety of soils. But for cultivation, clay loamy soil with large amount of humus and good drainage are supposed to be ideal. The pH of the soil should be acidic and around 4. The temperature range for cultivation is 10°C to 38°C. Rainfall should be in the range of 250 - 500 cm. Soils containing large amount of sand make the plants more susceptible to diseases.

It can be propagated by various methods, such as by seeds, roots, cutting, root stumps, etc. The propagation from seeds is usually the method of choice. The healthy seeds are sown into the nursery beds. The rate of germination of seeds is very low, hence sufficient quantity of the seeds are sown. Sowing is done in the month of May or at the break of monsoon. The seedlings are then transplanted in the month of August at a distance of 16 to 30 cm. The plants are provided with various chemical fertilizers and manures. The chemical fertilizers include ammonium sulphate, urea; while the manures include, generally, the bone-meal. The plants are kept free from weeds. When the plants are about 3 to 4 years old, they are uprooted. The roots are cut properly, washed so as to remove the earthy matter and dried in air.

It needs about 5 kg of seeds to produce the seedlings sufficient to cover the area of one hectare after transplantation. The average yield of roots per hectare is 1200 kg. It may vary, depending upon the soil, climatic conditions and age of the plant.

Macroscopic Characters (Figs. 2.26 and 2.27)

Colour - Root bark is greyish yellow to brown and wood, pale yellow.

Odour - Odourless

Taste - Bitter

Size - About 10 to 18 cm long and from 1 to 3 cm in diameter.

Shape - Roots are sub-cylindrical, slightly tapering and tortuous.

Fracture is short and irregular. The transversely cut surface is white, dense with finely radiating xylem.

Extra Features

Roots are rough with longitudinal marking and slightly wrinkled surface. Rootlets are usually absent, but few small circular root scars with tetrastichous arrangements are seen.

Fig. 2.26: Rauwolfia Twig

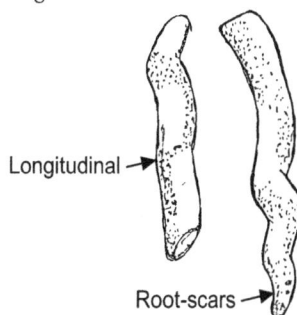

Fig. 2.27: Pieces of Rauwolfia Roots

Microscopic Characters (Fig. 2.28)

The cork is made up of stratified cells followed by phelloderm of few rows of parenchyma. Phloem is narrow, parenchymatous with small scattered sieve tissue. Parenchyma contains starch grains and few latex cells, with brown resinous matter. Secondary phloem contains calcium oxalate crystals. Xylem is about 4/5th of the diameter of the root and consists of vessels, tracheids, wood parenchyma and wood fibres. Xylem vessels are elongated up to 350 µ in length and 50 µ in width and contain simple or bordered pits. Stone cells and phloem fibres are absent.

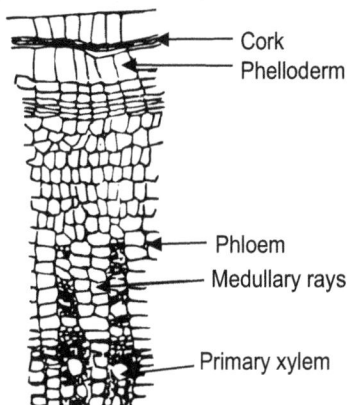

Fig. 2.28: T.S. of Rauwolfia Root

Chemical Constituents

About 30 indole alkaloids have been reported in drug and total alkaloidal content of rauwolfia roots ranges from 0.7 - 3 per cent, depending upon the source. Alkaloids are concentrated mostly in the bark of the roots. The alkaloids of rauwolfia are broadly classified into the following types, (a) indole alkaloids, (b) indoline alkaloids, (c) indolenine alkaloids (d) oxyindole alkaloids and (e) pseudo indoxyl alkaloids. The important alkaloid of rauwolfia is reserpine. Apart from the alkaloids, it also contains oleo-resin, phytosterol, fatty acids, alcohol and sugars. The other alkaloids present in the drug are ajmaline, ajmalicine, rauwolfinine, rescinnamine, reserpinine, yohimbine, serpentine and serpentinine. The major alkaloids reserpine and rescinnamine are esters derived from methyl reserpate and trimethoxybenzoic acid in reserpine and trimethoxycinnamic acid in case of rescinnamine. Syrosingopine is methyl carbethoxy syringoyl reserpate.

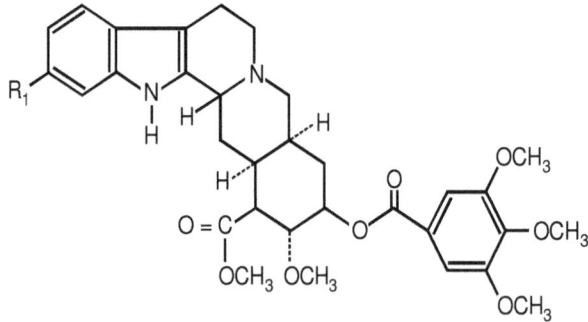

Deserpidine R₁ = H

Reserpine R₁ = OCH₃

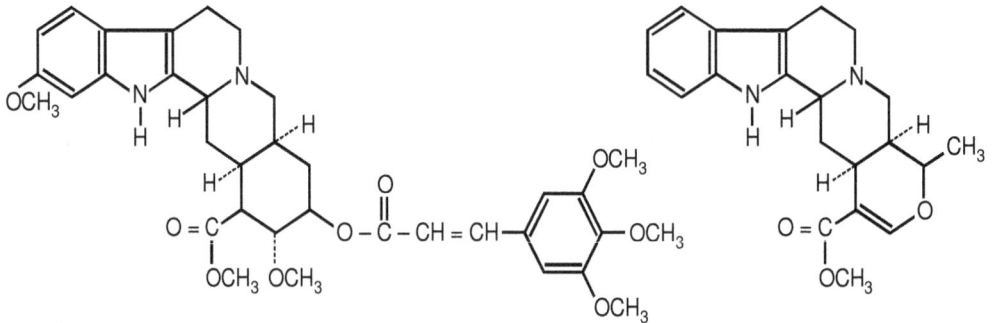

Rescinnamine　　　　　　　　　　　**Ajmalicine**

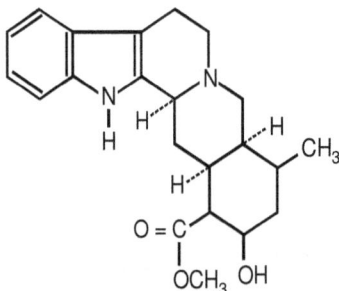

Yohimbine

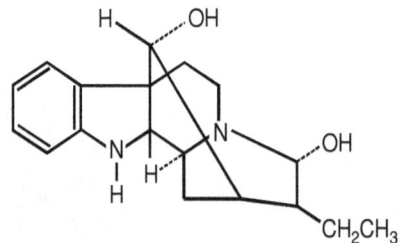

Ajmaline

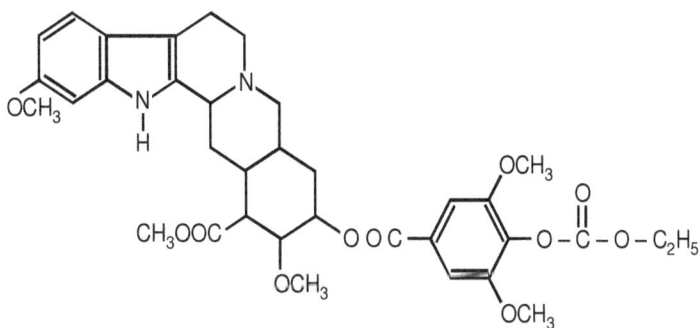

Syrosingopine

Reserpine like alkaloids is colorimetrically determined by reaction between acidic solution of alkaloids and sodium nitrite.

Chemical Tests

1. A red coloration along the medullary rays is observed when the freshly fractured surface is treated with concentrated nitric acid.

2. Reserpine shows violet red colour when treated with solution of vanillin in acetic acid.

3. Powdered ranwolfia when treated with sulphuric acid and p-dimethyl amino benzaldehyde, develops violet to red colour. (Test is for modle alkaloids).

Uses

Rauwolfia is antihypertensive in activity. Among the various alkaloids of rauwolfia, reserpine, rescinnamine and ajmalicine are clinically important. Reserpine lowers the blood pressure by depleting stores of catecholamines at nerve endings. It prevents re-uptake of nor epinephrine at storage sites, allowing enzymatic destruction of neuronal transmitter. It is used to treat mild essential hypertension and may be an effective adjunct to the treatment of more severe hypertension.

Because of the tranquillising effects, the drug is used in mild anxiety conditions and reserpine in some of the neuropsychiatric disorders.

Rescinnamine is also used as antihypertensive, but it causes mental depression in higher doses.

Deserpidine is used as antihypertensive and tranquilliser. It shows very less side effects.

Ajmalicine, though less in quantity, has the uses in treatment of circulatory diseases, in relief of obstruction of normal cerebral blood flow.

Syrosingopine shows peripheral effects similar to reserpine. It has less sedative actions and it is used for the treatment of mild or moderate hypertension.

Dose

Rauwolfia	:	100 to 150 mg (oral twice daily)
Reserpine	:	Initial dose 250 µg once a day (oral)
		Maintenance dose 100 - 250 µg once a day
Rescinnamine	:	500 µg oral twice a day (initial dose); 250 µg oral daily maintenance dose.

Allied Drugs and Substitutes

The rauwolfia species are not limited only to South East Asian region, but also found in Africa, Central and South America, New Guinea, Hawaii, New Caledonia, Australia and far east regions. It is reported that rauwolfia has about 86 different species. From the medicinal point, the most pertinent to mention here is *R. vomitoria,* which is known as African rauwolfia. It is used as a commercial source for the preparation of reserpine. The other known species of rauwolfia from Africa are *R. caffra, R. cumminsfi, R. mombasiana, R. oreogiton, R. obscura, R. rosea* and *R. volkensii.* All of them contain reserpine.

The other rauwolfia species with reserpine content are *R. tetraphylla* and *R. nitida. Catharanthus roses* contain ajmalicine.

Pausinystalia yohimba, known as yohimbe bark, contains yohimbine, which is structurally related to reserpine.

The root bark of *Alstonia venenata* and *A. constricta* also contain reserpine. The various species of *Aspidosperma* genus contain indole alkaloids which resemble to those from rauwolfia.

The various other species with which rauwolfia is found to be substituted are *Rauwolfia tetraphylla, R. densiflora* and *R. vomitoria* (African rauwolfia). *R. densiflora* contains sclerenchyma, while *R. tetraphylla* has uniform cork, abundant sclereids and fibres, but devoid of rescinnamine. The root of *R. vomitoria* has 5 discontinued bands of sclerenchyma and very large vessels.

CATHARANTHUS

Synonyms

Periwinkle, Vinca.

Biological Source

It is the dried whole plant of *Catharanthus roseus,* belonging to family Apocynaceae. It is also known as *Vinca rosea.*

Geographical Source

It is probably indigenous to Madagascar. It is cultivated in South Africa, India, U.S.A., Europe, Australia and Caribbean islands as an ornamental plant, as well as, for its medicinal properties.

History

Probably the use of vinca has been known since B.C. 50 in European countries as antidysentric, antihaemorrhagic, diuretic and wound healing. This plant was used in the form of 'tea' for treatment of diabetes in Jamaica and in Brazil for toothache. This plant was first scientifically investigated by Canadian workers Noble, Beer and Cutts. During these studies, it was found that it does not have any oral hypoglycemic principle, but contains alkaloid possessing antileukemic principle and the alkaloid was named as vincaleucoblastine. Because of such activity, the plant was thoroughly investigated at M/s Eli Lilly by Svoboda and his colleagues and they reported four dimeric indole alkaloids, viz. vinca-leucoblastine, leurosine, leurosidine and leurocristine. All these compounds exhibited anticancer activities. Some changes were later reported for the names of these compounds such as vincaleucoblastine to vinblastine and leurosine, leurosidine and leurocristine to vinleurosine, vinrosidine and vincristine respectively.

Cultivation, Collection and Preparation for the Market in India

Vinca grows all over India up to 500 metres. It is grown well in tropical and subtropical area in South Indian and North Eastern States of India. Except the highly alkaline or water-logged soil, vinca does not require any special conditions of soil. It favourably grows in light sandy soils, rich in humus. The rainfall of about 100 cm is most suitable for it. For the propagation, the fresh seeds are used and sown in nurseries or some times direct sowing is also done. For direct sowing, about 2.5 kg of seeds per hectare are required. They are mixed with 10 times quantity of sand and sown in monsoon in rows of 45 cm apart. When the plants are sufficiently grown up, they are thinned out and a distance of about 30 cm is left between two plants. Nursery sowing is found to be economical. In February or March, they are sown in nursery and transplanted in open fields after 2 months when they achieve 6 - 7 cm height. They are transplanted in open fields at 45 cm × 30 cm distance and about 74,000 plants per hectare are necessary. The plants do not need much water supply and are drought resistant. Though, the plant does not require any special supply of fertilizers, a mixture of nitrogen, phosphorus and potassium gives favourable results. Farmyard manure is also sometimes used. Weeding is done periodically and the leaf strippings are done 6 and 9 months after sowing. The stems are cut about 7 - 8 cm above the ground level after one year of growth and the leaves, stems and seeds are separated and air dried. For collection of roots, the field is profusely irrigated and roots are dug out by ploughing, which are further washed, dried in shades and packed in bales. The seeds are collected from matured fruits for next propagation. The yield of dried roots, stems and leaves per hectare in irrigated land is 1-5, 1 and 3 tones respectively.

As the plant contains very less percentage of alkaloids, it is not used as a galenical, but for extraction of the alkaloids. The extraction and separation procedure for alkaloids is based on their separation into soluble and insoluble tartarates in other solvents. Due to this vinblastine, vincristine and other weak bases are separated and then fractionated with the help of column chromatography, using alumina as adsorbent.

By using tissue culture technique, some of the vinca dimeric indole alkaloids like catharanthine and ajmalicine have been isolated. But yet, it has not, become the procedure for commercial utilisation. India is exporting vinca roots regularly. During 1989 - 90 and 1990 - 91, the exports were to the tune of ₹ 51.21 lakh and 83.15 lakh respectively.

Macroscopic Characters (Fig. 2.29)

The leaves are green, roots are pale grey, flowers are violet pink-white or carmine-red in colour. The odour is characteristic and taste is bitter. Vinca is an erect, pubescent herb, with branched tap-root. Leaves are simple, petiolate, ovate, or oblong, unicostate, reticulate, entire, brittle with acute apex and glossy appearance. Flowers are bractate, pedicellate, complete, hermaphrodite, normally 2 - 3 cm in cymose axillary clusters. Fruits are follicles with several black seeds.

Fig. 2.29: Vinca plant

Microscopic Characters (Fig. 2.30)

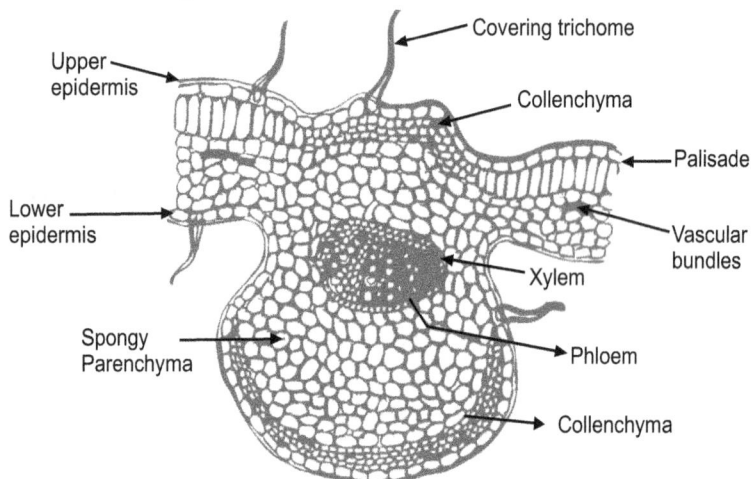

Fig. 2.30: T.S. of Vinca Leaf

Upper surface shows presence of single layer of rectangular celled epidermis with unicellular covering trichomes. Palisade is made up of single layer beneath upper epidermis and contains compact elongated cells. Spongy parenchyma is 5 - 8 layered with intercellular spaces. Midrib shows presence of collenchyma below the upper epidermis and above the lower epidermis. Xylem and phloem are present in the centre. Cruciferous stomata are present more frequently on lower epidermis. Calcium oxalate crystals are absent.

Chemical Constituents

A large number of indole alkaloids are present in vinca. Out of them, about 20 dimeric indole-dihydroindole alkaloids possess oncolytic activity, and among them, vincristine and vinblastine are most significant. Vinblastine contains indole alkaloid part called catharanthine and dihydroindole alkaloid part called vindoline. The other alkaloids present in vinca are ajmalicine, lochnerine, serpentine and tetrahydroalstonine. It requires about 500 kg crude drug to extract out 1 g of vincristine, because of its extreme low content, viz. 0.0002 per cent. This makes these alkaloids very costlier and hence, the efforts for their synthesis are under attempts. From their structure, the five-ring dihydroindole system is present in few other natural drugs. Therefore, the attempts towards the synthesis of four-ring indole system are going on presently. Such two systems can be further coupled.

Uses

Vinca is used to extract vincristine, vinblastine and ajmalicine. Vincristine sulphate is an antineoplastic agent which may act by arresting mitosis at the metaphase. It is given intravenously in the treatment of acute leukemia of children; some childhood leukemias are also responded. In adults, hodgkin's diseases, reticulum cell sarcoma, lymphosarcoma and myosarcoma have shown short remission.

Vinblastine sulphate is an antineoplastic agent, which may act by arresting mitosis at metaphase or by interfering with amino acid metabolism. It suppresses immune response and is mainly used in the treatment of hodgkin's disease and other lymphomas and choriocarcinoma. Vinca also exhibits hypotensive and antidiabetic actions.

Dose

1. Vincristine sulphate: 10 to 30 µg/kg of body weight intravenously, but maximum upto 2 mg.
2. Vinblastine sulphate: 100 µg/kg body weight intravenously.

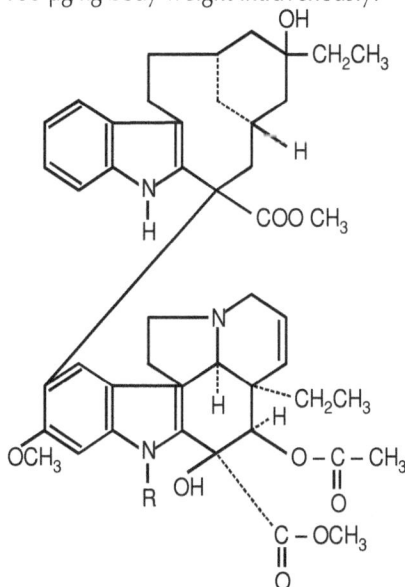

Vinblastine	**R = CH$_3$**
Vincristine	**R = CHO**

NUX VOMICA

Synonyms

Crow-fig, Semen strychni, Nux vomica seed.

Biological Source

Nux Vomica consists of dried ripe seeds of *Strychnos nux vomica* Linn, family Loganiaceae. It should contain not less than 1.2 per cent of total alkaloids calculated as strychnine.

Geographical Source

It is indigenous to East India and is largely collected from forests in Sri Lanka, Northern Australia and India. It is found abundantly in South India i.e. in Tamil Nadu, Kerala and on Malabar Coast. It is also available in the forests of Bihar, Orissa, Konkan, Mysore and Gorakhpur.

History

Because of its poisonous nature, this drug was used in sixteenth century to kill the animals. It is derived from a Greek word *Strychnos*, meaning poisonous and nux vomica indicates a nut with vomiting effects. Strychnine and brucine, the alkaloids present in this drug, are some of the few alkaloids which were first isolated. It was introduced in medical practice from 1640 onwards.

Collection

In India, the entire drug is collected from wild grown plants by the local tribal community. The nux vomica tree is found throughout the tropical area, 1300 m above the sea level. The plants are about 10 - 12 metres in height with a crooked trunk and several branches. The leaves are orange, oppositely arranged, with oval shape, entire margin and acute apex. The flowers are greenish-white and the bark is greyish to yellow. Fruits of the plants are orange yellow, berries of normal size. Each fruit contains about 4 - 5 seeds and heavy bitter pulp. The ripened fruits are collected and seeds are freed of the pulp. They are washed with water thoroughly. Unripened seeds are separated by the floating test in water. The seeds are dried on mat and packed in gunny bags for marketing. The collection of the fruit and seeds is carried out from November to February. In India, about 15,000 tones of seeds are collected annually. Seeds, pure and crude alkaloids of Nux-vomica are regularly exported from India. Exports of the alkaloids for 1988 - 89 and 1989 - 90 were ₹ 407.7 lacs and ₹ 429.5 lacs respectively.

Fig. 2.31: Nux Vomica Plant　　　　　　**Fig. 2.32: Nux Vomica Seed**

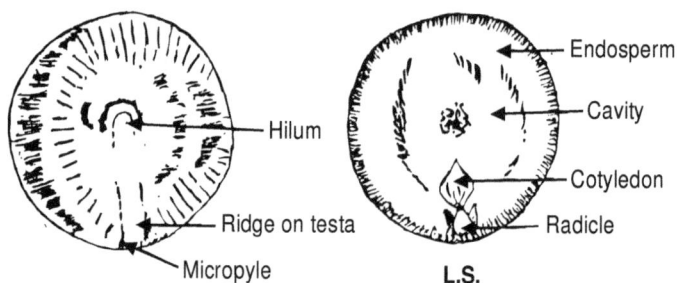

Macroscopic Characters (Figs. 2.31 and 2.32)

Colour　　-　Greenish-brown

Odour　　-　None

Taste　　　-　Intensely bitter

Size　　　-　Seeds are 10 to 30 mm in diameter and 4 to 6 mm in thickness.

Shape　　-　The seeds are disc shaped, somewhat flat or irregularly bent and concavo-convex. Margin of the seeds is rounded.

Extra Features

Surface of the seeds is silky due to the radially arranged, densely covered, closely appressed unicellular lignified covering trichomes. The presence of endosperm, embryo and cotyledons can be confirmed in the L. S. of the seed.

Microscopic Characters

The epidermis consists of strongly thickened, pitted and lignified trichomes. Epidermis is followed by a layer of collapsed cells. Endosperm is characterised by thick walled polyhedral unlignified cells with plasmodesma, aleurone grains and oil globules. Calcium oxalate crystals and starch grains are absent in drug (*Figs. 2.33* and *2.34*).

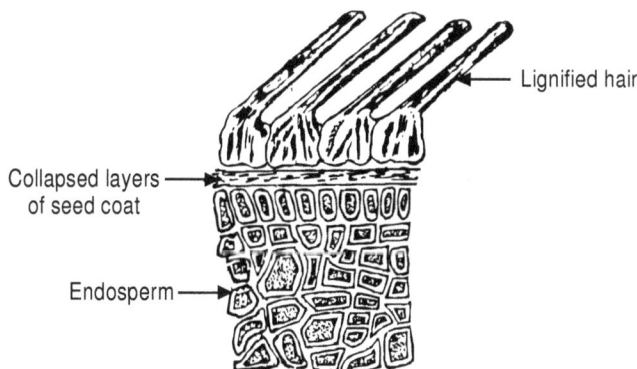

Fig. 2.33: T.S. of Nux vomica Seed

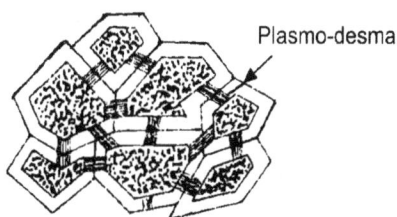

Fig. 2.34: Endospermic cells of Nux vomica Seed

Chemical Constituents

Nux vomica seeds contain 1.5 - 5 per cent of bitter indole alkaloids. Chief constituents of nux vomica are strychnine and brucine, while vomicine, α-colubrine, pseudostrychnine and strychnicine are also present. Apart from seeds, other parts of the plant contain alkaloids. Seeds also contain 3.0 per cent of fat. Bark contains brucine and traces of strychnine. Wood and root of the plant also contain strychnine.

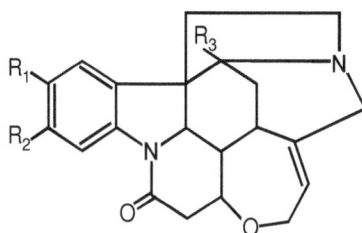

Strychnine	$R_1 = R_2 = R_3 = H$
Brucine	$R_1 = R_2 = ROCH_3, R_3 = H$
α - colubrine	$R_1 = H, R_2 = OCH_3, R_3 = H$
β - colubrine	$R_1 = OCH_3, R_2 = R_3 = H$

The other minor, but, chemically related alkaloids are isostrychnine, N-oxystrychnine, protostrychnine, β-colubrine, and novacine.

Nux vomica also contains a glycoside viz. loganin, chlorogenic acid and fixed oil.

The alkaloids can be isolated with the use of dilute sulphuric acid and lime. Strychnine sulphate is meagerly soluble in water and alcohol.

Chemical Tests

The thin sections of nux vomica seed are defatted and the following tests are performed.

1. Stain the transverse section of nux vomica with ammonium vanadate and sulphuric acid Manddin's reagent. The endospermic cells become purple due to the presence of strychnine.

2. Stain the transverse section of nux vomica with concentrated nitric acid. Endospermic cells take yellow colour due to the presence of brucine.

3. Strychnine with sulphuric acid and potassium dichromate gives violet colour which turns to red and finally yellow.

Uses

Due to its bitter taste, nux vomica is used as bitter stomachic and tonic. It is a stimulant to central nervous system. It increases the blood pressure and is recommended in certain forms of cardiac failure. It stimulates respiratory and cardiovascular systems. Brucine possesses very less physiological actions and is about one-sixth in potency as compared to strychnine. But as far as the bitterness is concerned, it is four times bitter than strychnine. Brucine is used for denaturing alcohol and inedible fats, as a standard for bitterness and as a dog poison.

During 1993-94 and 1994-95, India has exported nux vomica alkaloids of ₹ 443.5 lakhs and ₹ 230.8 lakhs.

Adulterants

1. Dried seeds of *Strychnos nuxblanda* Hill, are used as adulterant to nux vomica seeds. These are similar in size, pale in colour with a distinct ridge on the edge of the seeds. Nuxblanda seeds are regular in shape and contain traces of alkaloids.

2. Dried seeds of *Strychnos potatorum* are another adulterant to authentic drug. The seeds are also known as clearing nuts. They are smaller and thicker with yellowish buff colour. Seeds contain diaboline and traces of strychnine and brucine.

Allied Drugs

1. The seeds of *Strychnos wallichiana* are used as substitute to nux vomica, as their alkaloidal content and composition are comparable to the genuine drug.

2. The dried seed of *Strychnos ignatii* is another allied drug. Seeds are about 2.5 cm in diameter, ovoid in shape, dark green in colour with unlignified detached trichomes. It contains 2.5 per cent to 3 per cent alkaloids of which 60 per cent is strychnine. The seeds are used for the manufacture of strychnine.

PHYSOSTIGMA

Synonyms

Calabar bean, Ordeal bean

Biological Source

It is the dried ripe seed of *Physostigma venenosum* Balfour, belonging to family Leguminosae. It contains not less than 0.15 per cent of alkaloids of physostigma.

Geographical Source

West Africa, Gulf of Guinea

Macroscopic Characters (Fig. 2.35)

The drug is obtained from the legumes of perennial woody climber. The beans are flattened and reniform in shape with extremely hard, brown coloured. The testa of the seeds has a grooved hilum.

Chemical Constituents

The drug contains indole alkaloids, amongst which physostigmine, also called as eserine, is most important and it is present in the cotyledons.

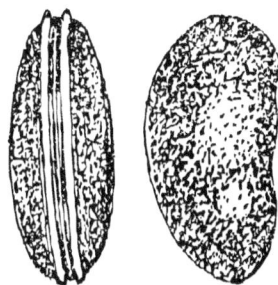

Fig. 2.35: Physostigma seeds

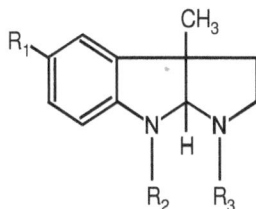

Physostigmine	$R_1 = CH_3 NHCOO$,	$R_2 = CH_3$,	$R_3 = CH_3$
Eseramine	$R_1 = CH_3 NHCOO$,	$R_2 = CH_3$,	$R_3 = CONHCH_3$
8-norphysostigmine	$R_1 = CH_3 NHCOO$,	$R_2 = H$,	$R_3 = CH_3$
Eseroline	$R_1 = OH$,	$R_2 = CH_3$,	$R_3 = CH_3$

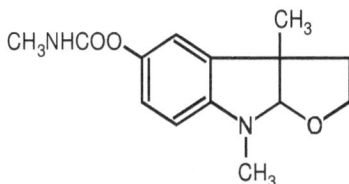

Physovenine

It is to be preserved properly from air and light as it is oxidized into rubeserine, a red compound, when exposed to air. Along with physostigmine, the drug also contains the alkaloids eseramine, geneserine, physovenine, calabatine, calabasine, isophysostigmine and N - 8 - norphysostigmine.

Uses

Physostigmine shows parasympathomimetic (ophthalmic) activity. It is categorised as an anticholinesterase agent. It enhances the cholinergic activity by inhibiting cholinesterase, and hence parasympathetic activity is sustained by physostigmine administration. It is used for contracting the pupils of the eye to counteract the poisoning caused by anticholinergic agents. It is also used as an antidote for reversing most of the cardiovascular (tachycardia and arrhythmia) and CNS effects due to overdosage with tricyclic antidepressants.

Dose

For ophthalmic purpose, topically 0.1 ml of 0.25 - 0.5 per cent solution.

For other purposes, intramuscularly or intravenously 1 - 4 mg slowly.

[6] IMIDAZOLE ALKALOIDAL DRUGS

PILOCARPUS

Synonym

Jaborandi.

Biological Source

The drug consists of the leaves of closely related plants of the genus *Pilocarpus*, belonging to family Rutaceae. The genus includes various species known by different names like *Pilocarpus jaborandi* (Pernambuco jaborandi), *P. pennatifolius* (Paraguay jaborandi), *P.microphyllus* (Maranham jaborandi), *P. trachylophus* (Ceara jaborandi), *P. selloanus* (Rio jaborandi), *P. spicatus* (Aracati jaborandi), *P. heterophyllus* (Barqui simento jaborandi) and *P. racemosus* (Guadeloupe).

Now-a-days, *P. microphyllus* i.e. Maranham jaborandi is the main source of this drug.

Geographical Source

It is indigenous to South America and especially grown in Brazil. It is found in Venezuela, Caribbean islands and Central America.

History

Dr. Coutinho in 1874 sent the plant to Europe from Pernambuco, hence the name Pernambuco jaborandi or Pilocarpus jaborandi. Later, Byasson in 1875 showed its alkaloidal nature and further Gerrard and Hardy isolated the main alkaloid pilocarpine.

Macroscopic Characters

The characters of main commercial variety, Maranham jaborandi are discussed here.

Jaborandi leaves are greyish green to greenish, brown in colour and have a slight aromatic odour along with bitter taste of alkaloids. When tested, the leaf causes increase in salivary secretion. It is an, imparipinnate compound leaf with 7 leaflets. The leaflets are asymmetrical, obovate and sessile in shape and 2 - 6 cm long and 1 - 3 cm wide in size. The terminal leaflet is symmetrical and oval in shape. The leaflets are present on the winged and glabrous rachis. The leaflet shows pinnate venation. They contain numerous oil cells.

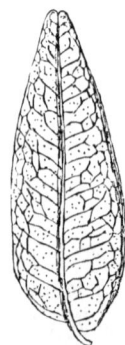

Fig. 2.36: A leaflet of Pilocarpus jaborandi

Chemical Constituents

The leaflets contain imidazole alkaloids among which pilocarpine is most important. Other alkaloids are isopilocarpine, pilocarpidine, pilosine, pseudopilocarpine, and isopilosine.

The range of total alkaloids in different species is between 0.5 to 1 per cent.

The oil cells observed in the leaf give volatile oil containing different monoterpenes like limonene, α - pinene, sabinene and sesquiterpenes.

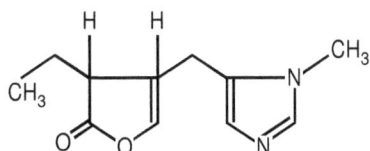

Pilocarpine

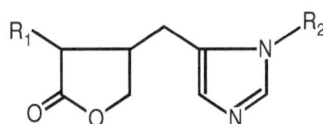

Pilocarpidine, $R_1 = C_6H_5$, $R_2 = H$
Pilosine, $R_1 = C_6H_5CHOH$,
$R_2 = CH_3$

Jaborandi Alkaloids

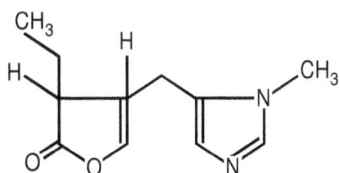

Isopilocarpine

The main alkaloid pilocarpine occurs as viscous oil or hygroscopic crystalline solid without any colour and odour. It is soluble in water and organic solvents, but insoluble in petroleum ether. It is the lactonic derivative of pilocarpic acid. The hydrolysis of pilocarpine results into pilocarpic acid, with loss of optical activity. Treatment with alkali produces isopilocarpic acid which is the stable stereoisomer. The alkaloids are totally deteriorated on long storage.

Chemical Test

To the pilocarpine solution, small quantity each of dilute sulphuric acid, hydrogen peroxide solution, benzene and potassium chromate solution is added. On shaking, organic layer gives bluish-violet colour and yellow colour appears in aqueous layer.

Uses

The drug is mainly used in the form of pilocarpine hydrochloride. It is a physiological antagonist of atropine. It acts directly on the autonomic effector cells of those structures innervated by post-ganglionic cholinergic nerves. Hence, it causes contraction of the pupil of the eye, and increase in sweating and salivation.

It is used in ophthalmology for the treatment of glaucoma.

Dose

Its recommended dosage is 0.05 - 0.1 ml of 10 per cent solution, topically.

[7] STEROIDAL ALKALOIDS

VERATRUM

Two important species of genus *Veratrum Veratrum viride* and *Veratrum album*. Both contain protoveratrine as active principle.

Veratrum contains two groups of alkaloids called jeveratrum and ceveratrum alkaloids. The alkamine part of both these groups is polyhydroxylated $C_{27}N$ fused polycyclic. The alkamines of jeveratrum group contain only 2 or 3 oxygen while in ceveratrum, they have 7 - 9 oxygen atoms. The members containing ceveratrum alkaloids are only therapeutically active, and their examples are cevadine, germerine, veratridine, protoveratrine A and protoveratrine B.

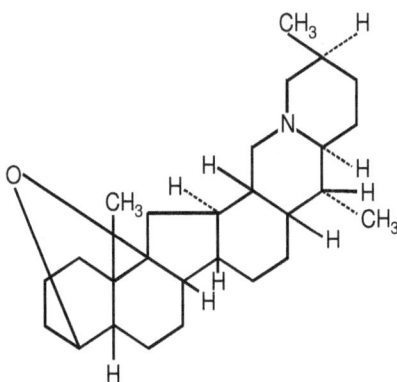

Ceveratrum nucleus

(a) Veratrum Viride

Synonyms

American or Green hellebore

Biological Source

It consists of dried rhizome and roots of *Veratrum viride* Aiton, belonging to family Liliaceae.

Geographical Source

The drug is obtained from wild growing plants in many parts of United States like states of New York, North Carolina, Georgia, Tennessee, etc. It is also found in some parts of Canada.

Macroscopic Characters

Colour	:	Brown
Odour	:	Unpleasant
Taste	:	Acrid
Size	:	Rhizomes are 5 - 8 cm in length and 2 - 3.5 cm in diameter
Shape	:	Subcylindrical with numerous stout yellowish brown roots.

It is a perennial about 1 - 2 m in height, large leaves, which are oral and strongly ribbed, star shaped many flowers in panicle.

Uses

The medicinal action is due to its many alkaloidal constituents. It lowers blood pressure and decreases heart rate. It used as a liquid extract or tincture in pregnancy associated hypertension.

(b) Veratrum Album

Synonym

White hellebore, European hellebore

Biological Source

It is the dried rhizome of *Veratrum album* Linne, belonging to family Liliaceae.

Geographical Source

It is native to Central and southern Europe, China and Japan.

Habitat

It is a decidous hardy perennial herb, flowers in June - July bears white flowers. Stem is hairy and 50 - 125 cm.

Macroscopic Characters

Colour   :   Brown

Odour   :   Unpleasant characteristic when fresh, dried with no odour

Taste   :   Burning, acrid and bitterish

Size   :   5 - 15 cm in length and 2 - 3 cm in diameter

Shape   :   Tuberous, fleshy with number of long white fibres at the end of the roots.

Fig. 2.37: *Veratrum album* plant

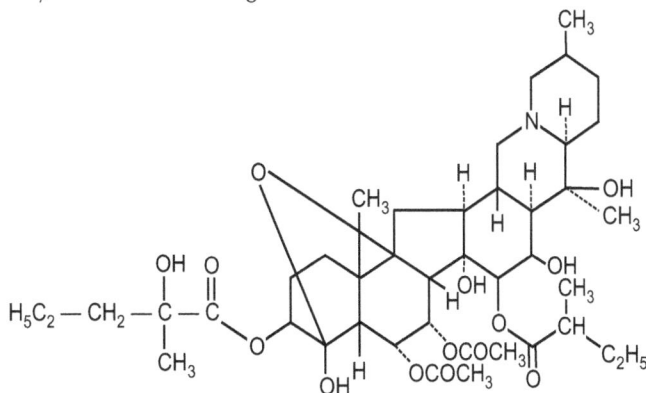

Protoveratrine A

Chemical Constituents

It contains mainly veratrine and also germidine, germitrine, protoveratrine, cevadine, pseudojervijne, veratrosine, etc.

Both Protoveratrine A and B are soluble in chloroform, but insoluble in water and light petroleum.

Uses

Veratrum album is mainly used as a source of protoveratrine A and B. Among these, protoveratrine A is medicinally more potent. They are used for the management of hypertension in pregnancy, especially in preclampsia and exclampsia conditions.

KURCHI

Synonym

Holarrhena

Biological Source

It is the dried stem bark of *Holarrhena antidysenterica* Wall belonging to family Apocynaceae. It is collected from 8 - 10 years old plant and freed from attached wood, and peeled into small pieces. It should contain not less than 2 per cent of total alkaloids of kurchi.

Geographical Source

Kurchi is indigenous to India and found throughout India in parts ascending up to 1000 metres in Himalayan region. It is also found in Orissa, Assam, Uttar Pradesh and Maharashtra.

Cultivation and Collection

The drug is obtained from wild source only. For the collection of bark, the plants which are 8 - 10 years old are selected. Longitudinal and transverse incisions are made on the trunk from July to September. After detachment, the bark is separated from the wood and dried. The recurved pieces of the bark are marketed.

Macroscopical Characters [Fig. 2.38 (a)]

Kurchi bark appears buff to pale brown on outer surface, while slightly brownish on inner surface. The outer surface is longitudinally wrinkled and bears horizontal lenticels. The pieces are recurved with varying size and thickness. The drug shows a short and granular fracture. It has no odour, but bitter and acrid taste.

(a) Kurchi twig fruiting　　　　(b) Pieces of Kurchi Bark　　　　(c) T. S. of Kurchi

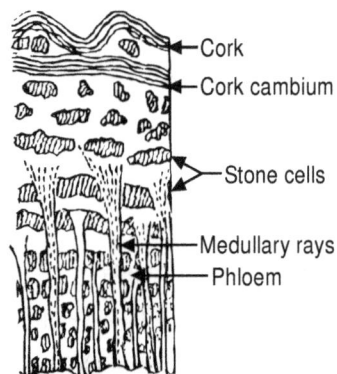

Fig. 2.38: Kurchi herb and bark

Microscopic Characters [Fig. 2.38 (c)]

In the periderm portion, cork has both tangentially and radially elongated cells. Cork cambium has several layers. Stone cells are present in cortex, either singly or in groups or in horizontal layers. It does not show phloem fibres. Phloem contains sieve tubes, companion cells, phloem parenchyma and stone cells. Medullary rays are multiseriate. In many stone cells, prismatic calcium oxalate crystals are present.

Chemical Nature

Kurchi contains about 25 total alkaloids (1.5 to 3 per cent). They are C_{21} group steroidal alkaloids. The active alkaloids are conessine (kurchicine), norconessine, isoconessine, dioxyconessine, conessimine, holarrhimine and holarrhidine.

Conessine is also present in root bark alongwith some other steroidal alkaloids.

Standards

    (1) Acid insoluble ash   - not more than 1 per cent

    (2) Alcohol (60 per cent) soluble   - 4 - 6 per cent

    (3) Foreign organic matter   - not more than 5 per cent

Uses

Kurchi is antiprotozoal in activity and used to treat amoebic dysentry. Conessine is highly active against *Entamoeba histolytica*. A traditional preparation of kurchi bark, viz. "kutajarishta" is commonly used, especially for chronic amoebiasis.

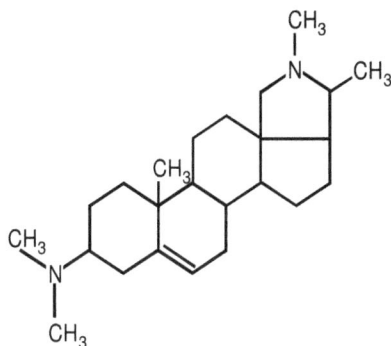

Conessine

[8] AMINO ALKALOIDS

EPHEDRA

Synonym

Ma-Huang

Biological Source

It consists of the dried young stems of *Ephedra gerardiana* (wall.) Stapf, and *E. nebrodensis* (Tineo.) Stapf, belonging to family Gnetaceae (Ephedraceae). Ephedra should contain not less than 1 per cent of total alkaloids, calculated as ephedrine.

Geographical Source

The main source of ephedra is from China, Pakistan, North-West parts of India, Australia, Kenya, Spain and Yugoslavia.

History

The drug originally belongs to Chinese System of Medicine. It has been used in China since last 5000 years. In Chinese language, it is called as Ma-Huang where 'Ma' denotes astrigent taste and 'Huang' is for yellow colour of drug. The references about this drug are found in the herbal of the emperor Shen Nung (2700 B.C.) and in 'Chinese medicinal plants' (1596 A.D.) by Pen T'sao Kang Mu. In those times, it was used for treatment of respiratory problems, fever and also for improving circulation. The drug was for the first time explored chemically by Yamanishi in Japan and he isolated ephedrine in crude form in 1885, which was further obtained in pure form by Nagai and Hari. Merck of Darmstadt, a German firm, carried out detailed search on *Ephedra helvectica* and isolated ephedrine in 1888. K. K. Chen and C. F. Schmidt are mainly credited for introduction of ephedra and ephedrine in modern therapeutics.

Cultivation, Collection and Preparation

Ephedra can be cultivated at an altitude of 2500 to 3000 m. Annual rainfall should not exceed 50 cm. It can be propagated by seeds or by layers or divisions of the root stock. Seeds are sown early in the spring at a distance of 5 cm, keeping the distance of one meter between 2 rows. The plants are collected after attaining the age of 4 years for the extraction of alkaloid. During this period, proper irrigation and weeding are necessary. The alkaloidal content of the drug varies from season to season. It is found to be maximum in autumn; when plants and twigs are dark in colour. Twigs are generally dried in sun or even by artificial ways. After drying, they are stored in dry and well closed containers, away from light.

Macroscopic Characters (Fig. 2.39)

Ephedra is a gymnospermous plant bearing thin stems which are woody, cylindrical and grey to greenish in colour (about 5 mm in diameter).

It shows the internodes at a distance of about 3 to 3.5 cm. Ephedra bears the scaly leaves from the nodes in a whorl of 2. The bases of the leaves are dark brown and they are joined on all sides of the node-forming a sheath. It bears a terminal bud, which is short and usually constricted at base. The male spikes are solitary, ovate, sessile and crowded.

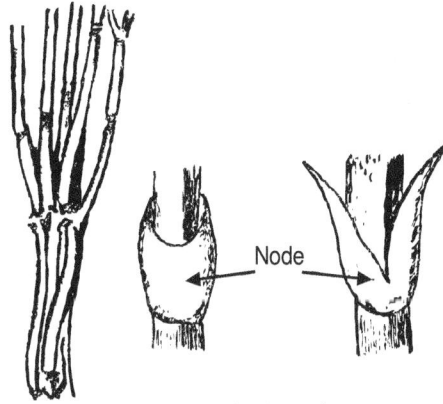

Fig. 2.39: Ephedra Twig

Microscopic Characters (Fig. 2.40)

The T.S. of ephedra shows the following characteristics.

(i) unicellular epidermis made up of quadrangular cells along with thick-walled cuticle,

(ii) vertical rows of sunken stomata and papillae on the ridges,

(iii) chlorenchymatous cortex,

(iv) non lignified, hypodermal fibres,

(v) lignified pericyclic fibres,

(vi) crystals of calcium oxalate in the cortex, and

(vii) parenchymatous dark brown coloured pith.

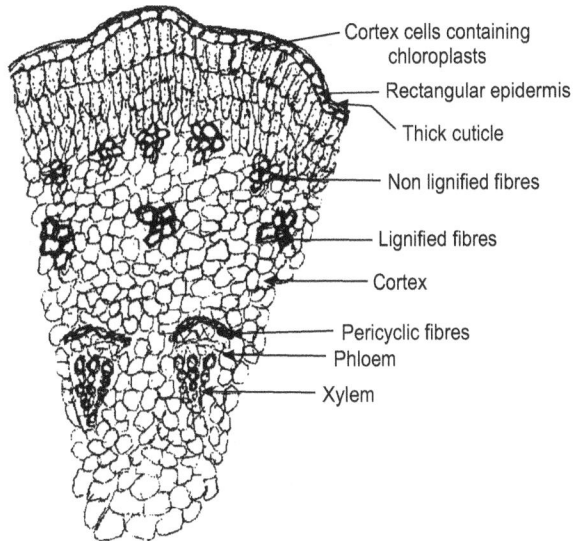

Fig. 2.40: T.S. of Ephedra Stem

Chemical Constituents

Ephedra contains the amino alkaloids. They are ephedrine, nor-ephedrine, n-methyl ephedrine, pseudo-ephedrine, etc.

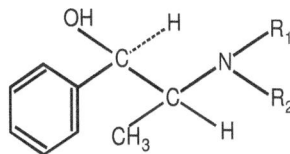

(−) Ephedrine	R_1 = H,	R_2 = CH_3
(−) Nor-ephedrine	R_1 = H,	R_2 = H
(−) n-methyl ephedrine	R_1 = CH_3,	R_2 = CH_3

Chemically, ephedrine ($C_{10}H_{15}$ NO) is 1-phenyl - 1 - hydroxy - 2 - methylaminopropane and is soluble in water, alcohol, organic solvents and oils. It is odourless and colourless, deliquescent and decomposes when exposed to air.

Along with the amino alkaloids, macrocyclic alkaloids called ephedradines are present in roots. The drug also contains oxazolidone.

Chemical Test

Ephedrine is dissolved in water and dilute hydrochloric acid and then treated separately with copper sulphate and sodium hydroxide. The solution gives violet colour. If shaken with solvent ether, the organic layer shows purple and aqueous layer shows blue colour.

Uses

Ephedra and its alkaloids show sympathomimetic effects. Hence, it is used as a bronchodilator in asthma and also in the treatment of allergic conditions like hay fever. As compared to adrenaline, the onset of action for ephedrine is slow, but the effect is much prolonged, as it is not quickly hydrolysed by mono amino oxidase in the body. Ephedrine is also used to correct the low blood pressure conditions, because of its peripheral contraction of arterioles. Ephedradines have hypotensive effects.

In 1995-96 and 1996-97, India has exported total ephedrine salts of worth ₹ 820.8 lakhs and ₹ 1555 lakhs respectively.

Dose

Ephedrine hydrochloride or sulphate 25 - 50 mg, 6 - 8 times a day, orally or parenterally and 0.1 ml 1 - 3 per cent solution, 2 - 3 times a day intravenously.

Other Species and Allied Drugs

The genus Ephedra has about 45 species, amongst which nearly 25 species contain ephedrine. The prominent species containing ephedrine are *E. equisetina and E. sinica* (both Chinese). *E. intermedia, E. major, E. helryetica and E. alata.* They contain from 35 - 87 per cent of ephedrine in total alkaloids. The other plants containing ephedrine are *Aconitum napelles* (Ranunculaceae); *Sida cordifolia*; and *S. rhombifolia* (Malvaceae); *Roemeria refracta* (Papaveraceae); and *Taxas baccata* (Taxaceae).

COLCHICUM

Synonyms

Meadow saffron seeds, Autumn crocus

Biological Source

It consists of the dried ripe seeds of *Colchicum luteum* Baker and *Colchicum autumnale* Linn, belonging to family Liliaceae. Colchicum corm is also used medicinally.

Geographical Source

It is found and cultivated in various parts of Europe, like England, Czechoslovakia, Holland, Poland and Yugoslavia. It is also cultivated in India (in Western Himalaya and Kashmir regions).

History

Though, it was known from the time of Dioscorides, it was not much used, owing to its toxic nature. In the medieaval times, Arabian people were using it for treatment of gout. It was reintroduced in European countries towards beginning of seventeenth century and first appeared in the London Pharmacopoeia in 1616. Pelletier and Caventou isolated colchicine in 1820.

Cultivation, Collection and Preparation

In nature, colchicum propagates by repeating the life cycle with the corm which is present as a swollen underground stem with sheathing leaves. Towards the end of summer, the fully grown corm develops daughter corms in the axil of scaly leaf near the base. These daughter corms develop parasitically on parent corm and subsequently, the parent corm withers away. After this, the daughter corms develop into new plants.

In Jammu and Kashmir and different parts of Europe and Africa, the drug is obtained by propagation with seeds. The propagation is done by sowing the seeds in boxes at an altitude of 1000 - 3000 m. The seedlings are transplanted in open fields at a distance of 1 m. The plants bear the capsular fruits after one year of vegetative growth. The fruits are collected before dehiscence and dark seeds are separated, processed and graded. The corms are isolated and the adhering scales and coats are removed. The corms are sliced transversely and dried below 65°C.

Macroscopic Characters (Fig. 2.41)

(a) Colchicum Seeds

Colchicum seeds are very hard in nature and show a reddish-brown testa. The seeds have a projection at the hilum and from there develops strophiole, which is an outgrowth of testa. The seeds are 2 - 3 mm in diameter, having bitter and acrid taste and no odour. The corms are 2 - 3 cm in diameter and used in the sliced form which are reniform and ovate in shape, with 2 - 5 mm, thickness. They have a short fracture, bitter taste and no odour.

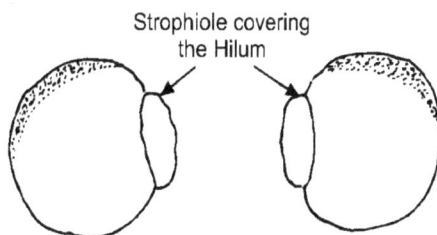

Strophiole covering the Hilum

Fig. 2.41: Colchicum Seeds

(b) Colchicum Corms

Colour	: Yellowish-brown
Odour	: none
Taste	: bitter and acrid
Size	: slices are about 2 - 5 mm in thickness
Shape	: sub-reniform or ovate in outline or
Extra features	: Fracture is short and cut surfaces are white and starchy, showing greyish points.

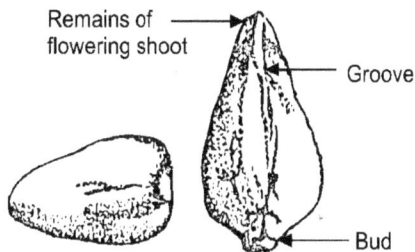

Remains of flowering shoot

Groove

Bud

Fig. 2.42 : Colchicum Corms

Microscopic Characters

The section of seed shows parenchyma and endosperm. The parenchymatous cells are reddish-brown with thick walls. The endospermic cells show pitted walls and contain aleurone grains and fixed oil. The strophiole portion of seed contains starch.

The corm has epidermis, parenchyma and vascular tissue. The parenchymatous cells have abundant starch grains. The epidermis has circular stomata. In vascular part, the xylem vessels are spiral or annular.

Chemical Constituents

Colchicum seed contains 0.2 - 1 per cent of amino alkaloids of which colchicine is the main constituent. The seeds contain upto 0.8 per cent of colchicine and in corms, it is upto 0.6 per cent. Colchicum also contains demecolcine. Both the alkaloids contain tropolone or cycloheptatrien-ol-one ring structure.

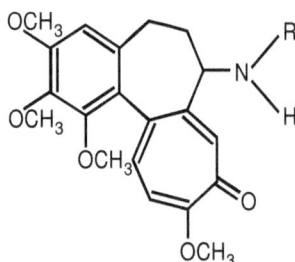

Colchicine, R = COCH$_3$,　　　Demecolcine, R = CH$_3$

Colchicine ($C_{22}H_{25}O_6N$) is obtained as pale yellow crystals, amorphous or in powder form. It has a bitter taste and is odourless. It darkens on exposure to air. Colchicine is freely soluble in alcohol and chloroform, soluble in 25 parts of water and in 220 parts of solvent ether.

Chemical Tests

(1) Colchicine gives yellow colour with 70 per cent sulphuric acid.

(2) Alcoholic solution of colchicine, when treated with ferric chloride gives red colour.

Uses

Colchicum is a specific drug for treatment of gout and rheumatism. Colchicine also possesses antitumour activity.

Apart from medicinal use, colchicine is widely accepted and practised as a chemical agent for bringing the polyploidy (increase in number of chromosomes) and hence used in horticulture and cultivation of medicinal plants.

Dose

Colchicine:　　500 – 650 µg, orally 1 - 3 times a day, orally

　　　　　　　　500 µg to 1 mg,1 - 2 times a day, intravenously

Allied Drugs

The plants having chemical contents similar to colchicine type of alkaloids belong to different genera, such as *Dipidax, Gloriosa, Androcybium, Camptorrhiza,* etc.

The other genera in which colchicine is present are from the same family Liliaceae, like *Androcymbium, Bulbocodium, Dipidax, Littonia, Fritillaria, Ornithoglossum,* etc. and *Narcissus* and *Crocus* from families Amaryllidaceae and Iridaceae respectively.

[9] PURINE ALKALOIDAL DRUGS (PURINES)

Fusion of 6-membered pyrimidine ring to a 5-membered immidazole ring results in Purine derivatives. As such, purines do not occur in nature but many purine derivatives play significant role biologically. They are very closely related to purine bases adenine and guanine, which are the fundamental components of neucleic acids.

Pharmaceutically important purine bases are xanthines i.e. methylated derivatives of 2-6 di-oxy purines.

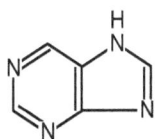   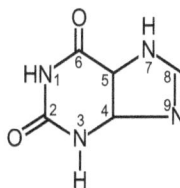

Purine   **Xanthine**

Few medicinally important xanthines are:

1) Caffeine: is 1, 3, 7 trimethyl xanthine

2) Theophylline is 1, 3 dimethyl xanthine

3) Theobromine is 3, 7 dimentyl xanthine

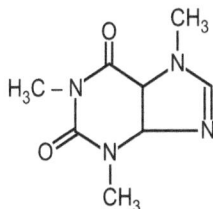   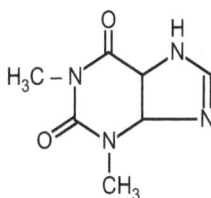   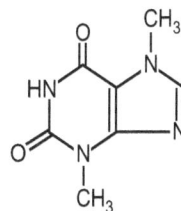

Caffeine   **Theophylline**   **Theobromine**

COFFEE

Synonyms

Coffee bean, coffee seed.

Biological Source

It is the dried ripe seed of *Coffea arabica* Linne or *C. liberica* Hiern, and deprived of most of the seed coat. It belongs to family Rubiaceae.

Geographical Source

It is found in Ethiopia, Brazil, India, Vietnam, Mexico, Guatemala, Indonesia and Sri Lanka.

Coffee beverage is popular in different parts of world. The amount of caffeine present is also more than in tea. In middle east countries, it is known by name 'qahuah'. It is a strong decoction of coffee seed powder. The word has its origin in Turkish and Arabic languages. The major suppliers of coffee, now-a-days, are Brazil and India. Karnataka, Kerala and Tamil Nadu grow large plantation of coffee. (*Fig. 2.43*). At present it is cultivated in Maharashtra also.

Habitat

Coffee plant is an evergreen shrub which bears drupe type of fruit with an ellipsoidal or spheroidal shape. Each fruit has 2 locules, with one seed in each chamber. Each plant gives about 2 - 3 kg of coffee seeds. The fruits are dried to separate the seeds. The seeds are separated by wetting them and mechanically separating, followed by drying in heaps, which causes fermentation.

The separated seeds or beans are green in colour. They are roasted by which the colour and odour is effected. The seeds acquire dark brown colour and possess an agreeable odour and bitter taste.

India produced 1.65 and 2.35 lakh tones of coffee during 1998 - 99 and 99 - 2000 respectively.

Fig. 2.43: Coffee Plant with fruits

Chemical Constituents

The main constituents of coffee bean are caffeine, tannin, fixed oil and proteins. It contains 2 - 3 per cent caffeine, 3 - 5 per cent tannins, 13 per cent proteins, 10 - 15 per cent fixed oils, chlorogenic or caffeotannic acid and sugars in the form of dextrin, glucose, etc. In the seeds, caffeine is present as a salt of chlorogenic acid. During roasting process, the agreeable smell of coffee is developed which is due to an oil called caffeol composed of mainly furfural alongwith minor quantities of phenol, pyridine and valerianic acid.

Extraction of Caffeine

Caffeine is prepared either by synthesis (from urea or uric acid) or extracted from natural sources. Coffee bean is one of the major sources for it. For the extraction, coffee roasters are used in which caffeine sublimed during roasting is recovered. It is the commercial method for extraction of caffeine.

Uses

It is used as a source of caffeine. The main effects of coffee i.e. stimulant and diuretic actions are due to caffeine. It is, sometimes, used to combat the toxic effects due to CNS depressant drugs. During 1997 - 98 and 98 - 1999 India exported coffee worth of ₹ 17.07 and 17.51 crores respectively.

Other Preparations

Decaffeinated coffee: This product has been introduced in developed countries. It has been specially designed, because of addiction effects of coffee. It has all the agreeable odour of coffee beans, but contains a meagre amount (about 0.08 per cent) of caffeine.

COLA

Synonyms

Kola nut, Cola nut.

Biological Source

This consists of matured and dried seeds of the plant, *Cola acuminata* or Cola nitida family: Sterculiaecae.

Geographical Source

Tropical rain forests of Africa, Sierra Leone and Congo, Sri Lanka, Brazil, Indonesia and West Indies. It is propagated through seeds. It is a evergreen tree of 20 metres, has long ovoid leaves which are pointed at both the ends. The leaves have leathery texture and bear yellow flowers with purple sports. It bears chocolate coloured pods about 5 – 10 cm in length which accommodates about 10 to 12 seeds. Seeds are removed from fruits, their onter coating is removed and the bare cotyledons are collected. They are dried in Sun immediately. Cola nuts tend to mold and spoil easily, hence dried thoroughly. Only processed colidons are exported to market.

Macroscopic Characters

Colour : Seeds are chocolate brown in colour.

Odour : Bitter flavour, aromatic and rose like.

Taste : Bitter in the beggening and some what sweetish.

Shape : Seeds are round or square shaped.

Chemical Constituents

Kola nuts contain upto 3.5% of caffeine and less than one per cent theobromine. The alkaloids are bound with tannin i.e. Kolacatechin in seeds.

Fig. 2.44: Cola acuminata herb

Uses

Due to caffeine kola seeds are stimulant and therefore are the ingredients in carbonated beverages. Kola nut are also used to treat whooping cough and asthma, due to bronchodiating effect of caffeine.

TEA

Synonym

Camellia thea

Biological Source

It contains the prepared leaves and leaf buds of *Thea sinensis* (Linne) O. kuntze, belonging to family Theaceae (Ternstroemiaceae).

Geographical Source

Large areas of land are put under cultivation of tea in India, Sri Lanka, China, Indonesia and Japan. It is available as **black tea** from India and Sri Lanka and **green tea** from China and Japan.

Black tea is obtained by fermenting the heap of fresh tea leaves and further drying with artificial heat. **Green tea** is obtained by putting tea leaves in copper pans and then drying by artificial heat.

Macroscopic Characters

It is a small evergreen shrub when cultivated reaches to the height of 1.0 - 1.5 metres, while wild growing plants reach upto 6.0 metres. Plant is much branched and bears grey bark.

Fig. 2.45: Twig of tea-herb

Leaves: Dark green, lanceolate or elliptical, blunt at apex, base is tapering margin shortly serrate. Young leaves are hairy while matured leaves are glabrous.

Flowers are solitary or in groups of 2 or 3 in the leaf axils, and drooping.

Odour : Characteristics

Taste : Bitter

Preparation of Green Tea

It is prepared by exposing the freshly collected leaves to the air until most of the moisture is removed. Then they are roasted and stirred continuously until leaves become moist and flaccid. Then they are passed to rolling table and rolled into balls and subjected to a pressure which removes the moisture. Then the leaves are shaken out on the copper pans and roasted again till the leaves assume dull green colour. Then the leaves are winnowed, screened and graded into various varieties.

Chemical Constituents

Tea leaves are considered as a rich source of caffeine (1 - 3 per cent). It is extracted from tea dust and tea leaf waste or sweepings. It also contains theobromine and theophylline in minor quantities. The colour of tea leaves is due to gallotannic acid (15 per cent). The agreeable odour is due to presence of a yellow volatile oil. Tea leaves also contain an enzymatic mixture called thease.

Use

Tea is useful as a CNS stimulant in the form of beverage besides, it is a diuretic as well.

[10] QUINAZOLINE ALKALOIDAL DRUGS

VASAKA

Synonyms

Adhatoda, Adulsa, Malabar nut.

Biological Source

It consists of dried, as well as, fresh leaves of the plant *Adhatoda vasica* Nees, belonging to family Acanthaceae, and contains not less than 0.6 per cent of vasicine on dried basis.

Geographical Source

Vasaka is indigenous to India, where it is found in sub-Himalayan track up to an altitude of 1000 m, and in Maharashtra especially, in Konkan region. Besides India, it is found in Myanmar, Sri Lanka and Malaya.

Cultivation and Collection

The uses of vasaka have been known since old times and it is included in different formulations of ayurveda.

The plant is not cultivated on commercial scale. It is obtained from garden plants or wild sources. It can be easily propagated by stem cuttings and by seed germination. The plant is obtained in all seasons of the year. It reaches to a height of 2 - 3 metres. It is also observed that the plant favourably grows in loamy soil.

Fig. 2.46: Vasaka herb

Macroscopic Characters

The drug contains stem leaf, fruit and seeds. The leaves have 10 - 30 cm length and width of 4 - 10 cm. They are petiolate and exstipulate. The shape is lanceolate. The margin is crenate with acuminate apex. There are 8 - 10 pairs of lateral veins. Taste is better and odour is characteristic.

Microscopic Characters (Fig. 2.47)

The epidermis shows caryophyllaceous stomata with sinuous epidermal cells, and covering and glandular trichomes. It is a dorsiventral leaf with palisade having 2 layers of cells. 2 - 3 bicollateral vascular bundles are seen in midrib. Mesophyll contains prismatic and acicular crystals of calcium oxalate. Stomatal index is from 10.8 - 18.2 and palisade ratio from 5 - 8.5.

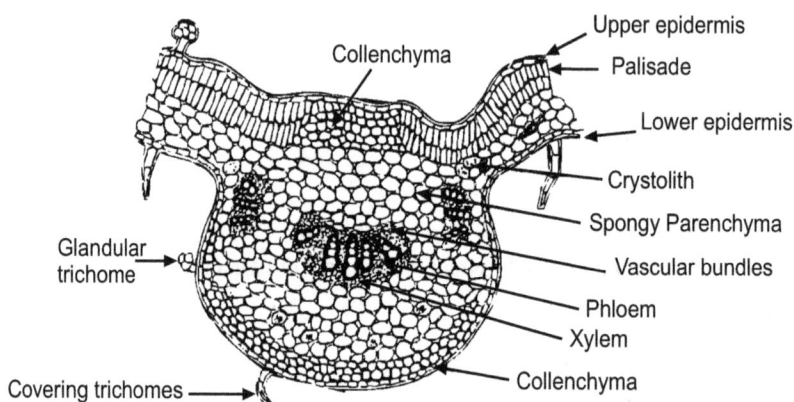

Fig. 2.47: T.S. of Vasaka leaf

Chemical Constituents

Vasaka leaves contain quinazoline derivatives such as vasicine 2.0 to 2.5 per cent, vasicinone and 6-hydroxy vasicine. Biochemically, vasicine is oxidised to its ketonic derivative vasicinone and the latter exerts main activity as bronchodilator. The drug also contains volatile oil, betain and vasakin. It is also reported that vasaka contains adhatodic acid, adhatodine and vasicol.

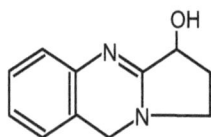

Vasicine

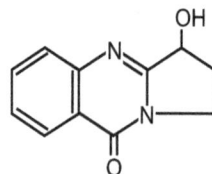

Vasicinone

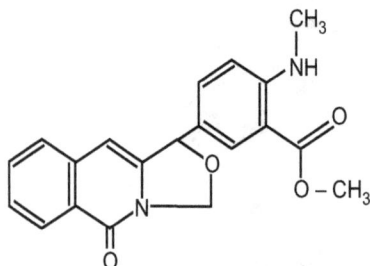

Adhatodine

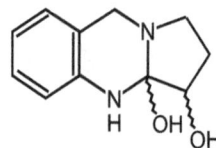

Vasicol

Standards

Foreign organic matter - not more than 2 per cent.

Uses

Vasaka is used as expectorant and bronchodilator. The large doses are irritant and cause vomitting and diarrhoea. The pharmacological investigations have shown that vasicine also shows oxytocic property similar to oxytocin and methyl ergometrine. Vasicine also shows abortificient action and both the actions are due to release of prostaglandins. Bromhexine HCl is a synthetic derivative of vasicine which changes the structure of bronchial secretions and reduces viscosity of sputum. It does not cause drowsiness or dependance.

[11] DITERPINOIDAL ALKALOIDS

Nitrogen containing Diterpenoidal bases have been isolated from various plant families. Specially Runanculaceae, Rosaceac, Escalloniaceae. The complex structure with C_{19} to C_{20} (carbon) atoms are refered as norterpenoid or diterpenoid alkaloids.

ACONITE

Synonyms

Aconite root, Bachnag, Monkshood.

Biological Source

It is the dried root of *Aconitum napellus* Linn belonging to family Ranunculaceae. It should contain not less than 0.6 per cent of alkaloids of aconite, of which not less than 30 per cent should be aconitine.

Geographical Source

Aconite is found is Hungary, Germany, Spain and Switzerland. It is cultivated in England. In India, it is collected from wild or cultivated plants and the drug collected is *A. chasmanthum* or *A. ferox*.

Macroscopic Characters (Fig. 2.48)

The roots are dark brown in colour, with a slight odour. It has a slight taste which causes tingling sensation followed by numbness of tongue. They are 4 - 10 cm in length and 1 - 3.5 cm in width. Roots are broad towards the crown and tapering towards the distal end. The fracture is short and horny. The roots are slightly twisted and deeply wrinkled. The broader end of the root bears numerous rootlets and scars. The daughter roots are the diagnostic characters of parent roots.

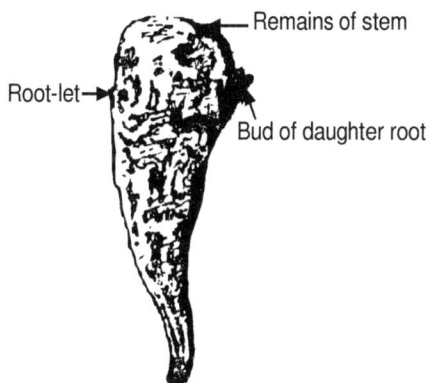

Fig. 2.48: Aconite root

Chemical Constituents

Aconite contains diterpene alkaloids like aconitine, hypoaconitine, neopelline, napelline, neoline and traces of sparteine and ephedrine. Among them only aconitine is the most important, having poisonous action. The chief constituent of drug is aconitine and is ether-soluble. The ether-soluble alkaloids vary in different species of aconite. The drug also contains aconitic acid, succinic acid and starch.

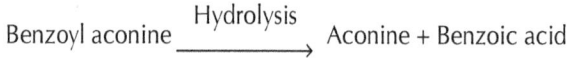

$$\text{Aconitine} \xrightarrow{\text{Hydrolysis}} \text{Benzoyl aconine} + \text{Acetic acid}$$

$$\text{Benzoyl aconine} \xrightarrow{\text{Hydrolysis}} \text{Aconine} + \text{Benzoic acid}$$

The products of hydrolysis are less active.

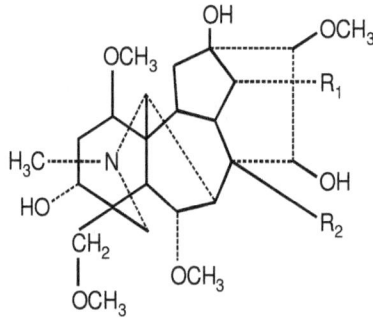

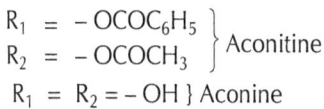

$$R_1 = -OCOC_6H_5$$
$$R_2 = -OCOCH_3 \bigg\} \text{ Aconitine}$$
$$R_1 = R_2 = -OH \} \text{ Aconine}$$

Standards

1. Ash   - not more than 5 per cent
2. Acid-insoluble ash   - not more than 1 per cent
3. Aerial stem   - not more than 5 per cent
4. Foreign organic matter   - not more than 2 per cent

Uses

It is a highly poisonous drug. It is used externally (in the form of liniment) in the treatment of neuralgia, sciatica, rheumatism and inflammation. It is also analgesic and cardiac depressant. Now-a-days, its use is restricted only to homeopathic medicines.

Substitutes

1. Japanese aconite A. unicinatum.
2. Indian aconite A. chasmanthum.

❖❖❖

Chapter 3...

STEREOISOMERISM AND NATURAL PRODUCTS*

It is very essential to know the terminology used to describe the phenomenon of stereoisomerism. Basic terms are to be defined precisely with sufficient number of examples. The examples quoted in every activity are from natural products only. i.e. menthol, carvone, erythrose, geraniol etc.

HISTORY OF STEREOCHEMISTRY

The credit for study of stereochemistry goes to **Louis Pasteur**. He is called as first stereochemist. **Pasture in 1849** found that tartaric acid salt obtained from the wine production vessels rotates the plane of polarized light. But, tartaric acid salt obtained from other sources does not rotate the plane of polarized light. The two types of tartaric acid salts differ on the basis of optical isomerism.

Jacobus Henricus Van't Hoff and Joseph Le Bel described the optical activity in the view of the tetrahedral arrangement of the atoms bound to carbon. **Cahn –Ingold –Prelog sequence rule** priority is used to guess the molecular stereochemistry. Later, **Fischer** projection in a very easy way could explain the stereochemistry around the stereocenter.

Stereochemistry

It is a branch of chemistry. Stereochemistry is defined as the three dimensional chemistry as the prefix "stereo-" means "three-dimensionality". It deals with the relative special arrangement of atoms which forms structure of molecule and its manipulation. An important area in the stereochemistry is chiral study and stereoisomers.

Optical Activity

The substance which rotates the plane of polarized light is called as **optically active** substance.

Plane Polarized light

It is a light whose vibration takes place in only one of different possible planes. Ordinary light can be converted into plane polarized light by passing it through Nicol Prism.

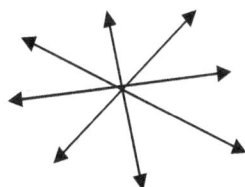

Ordinary light   Plane polarized light

---

* This chapter has been written by Dr. SHIRKHEDKAR A.A., RC Patel College of Pharma-Education and Research, SHIRPUR 425 405 (M.S.)

Chiral carbon

It is defined as a carbon atom to that four different atoms or groups are attached. It is also called as chiral carbon. It is denoted by * Asterisk on carbon atom i.e. C*. **e.g.**

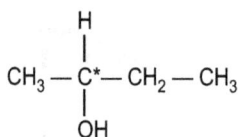

$$CH_3 - \overset{\overset{\displaystyle H}{|}}{\underset{\underset{\displaystyle OH}{|}}{C^*}} - CH_2 - CH_3$$

* indicating chiral centre

Butan-2-ol

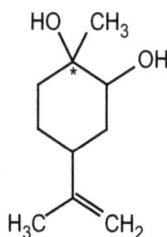

* indicating chiral centre in

Limonene 1, 2-diol

Isomers

It is defined as molecules that have the identical molecular formula but the different structural arrangement of the atoms.

Isomers Classification

Isomers are broadly classified into :

1) **Structural isomers :**
    (i) On the basis of arrangement of carbon skeleton
    (ii) On the basis of position of functional groups
    (iii) On the basis of diverse functional groups
2) **Stereoisomers:** It is also called as spatial isomers
    (i) Configurational
        A. Geometric
        B. Optical
            (a) Enantiomers
            (b) Diastereomers
    (ii) Conformational

1. Structural isomerism

It is also called constitutional isomers. It has same molecular formula but the bonded Links and /or their order differ between different atoms or groups.

2. **Stereoisomers**

These are the isomeric molecules which posses the identical molecular formula and sequence of bonded atoms, but they differ only in the three dimensional orientations of their atoms in the space. In stereoisomerism the order and bond links of the constituent atoms remain the same, but their arrangements in the space differs.

Configuration

The arrangement of atoms that characterizes a particular stereoisomer is called its configuration.

Optical isomerism

It is a form of stereoisomerism. These molecules vary in only characteristic i.e. their interaction with plane polarized light.

If the plane polarized light is passed through solution of compound and if rotates plane polarized light in clockwise direction or right side then it is called as **dextro rotatory** compound or dextro form or (+) form.

Example: (+) alanine; d- alanine

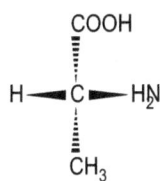

(+)- alanine

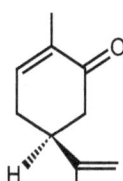

(+)-Carvone

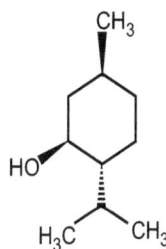

(+) Menthol

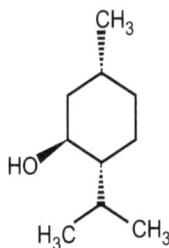

(+)-Isomenthol

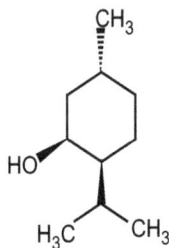

(+) -Neomenthol

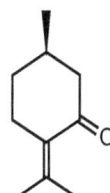

(+) -Pulegone

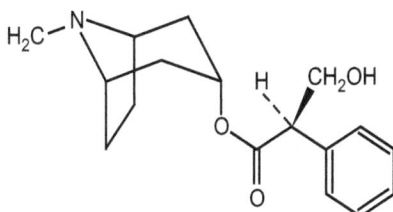

(+)-Hyoscyamine

If the plane polarized light is passed through solution of compound and if that rotates plane polarized light in anticlockwise direction or to left side then it is called as **levorotatory** compound or levo form or (–) form.

Example

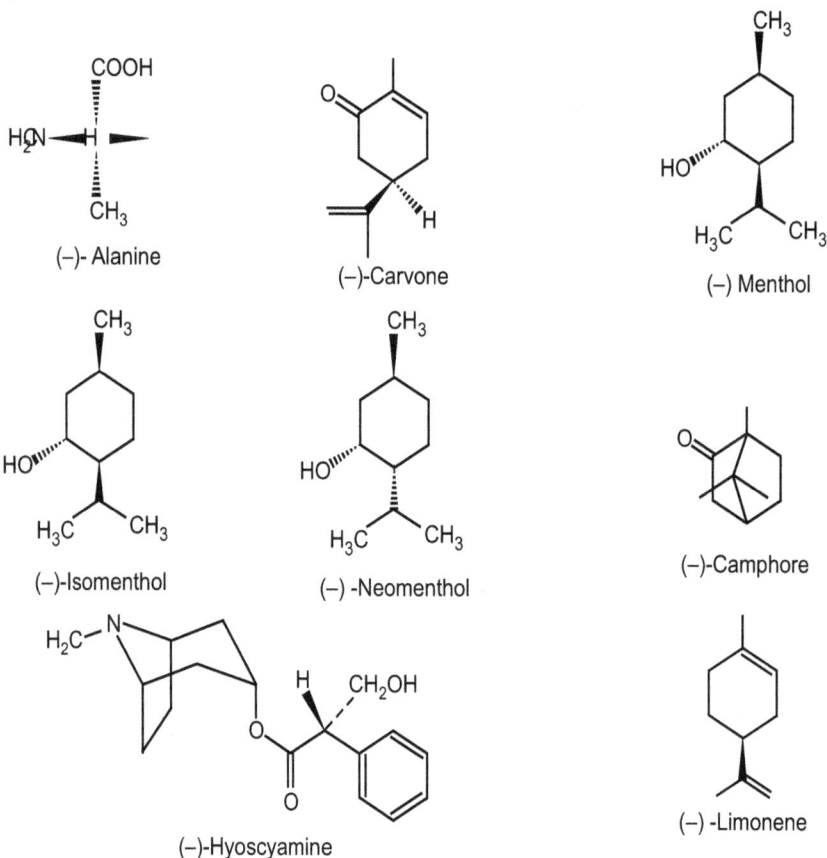

(–)- Alanine

(–)-Carvone

(–) Menthol

(–)-Isomenthol

(–) -Neomenthol

(–)-Camphore

(–)-Hyoscyamine

(–) -Limonene

Racemic Mixture

It is also called as racemate. It is having equivalent proportions of left and right handed enantiomers of chiral molecule. It contains 50 : 50 percentage of dextro- and levo isomeric form of the molecule. Racemates are optically inactive i.e no fixed rotation of plane polarized light. It is represented by keeping (**±**) **or dl- or DL-** for sugars in front of the name of the compound. If the dextro and levo isomers are not in equal proportions then it can be represented by prefix (**+**) /(**–**) **or d/l or D/L-.** Racemates may dissimilar in properties than the any one of the pure enantionmers.

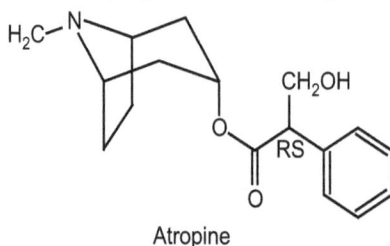

Atropine

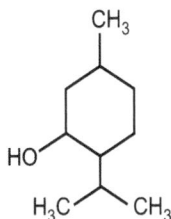

(±-Racemic mixture of
menthol isomers

Enantiomers

These are defined as isomers that are mirror images of each other. They are non super-imposable i.e. not identical.

Organic compound containing a chiral carbon generally have two non-superimposable structures. These two structures are mirror images of each other and thus commonly known as enantiomorphs.

Enantiomers have similar chemical properties. Enantiomers have similar physical properties apart from that they have different capacity to rotate the plane of polarized light by equal amounts but in the opposite direction.

Example

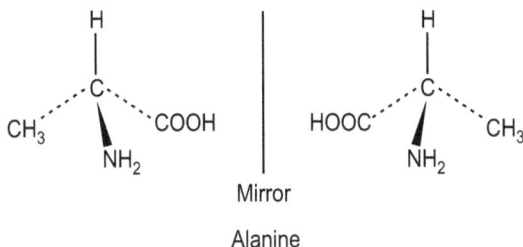

Mirror

Alanine

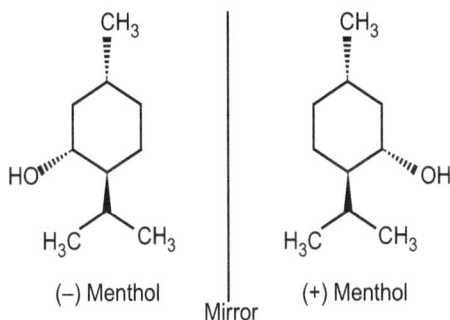

(−) Menthol   (+) Menthol

Mirror

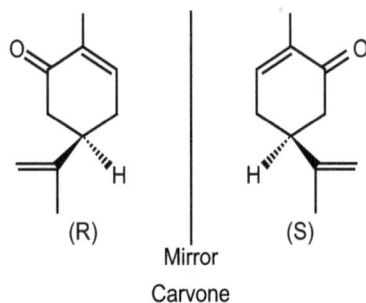

(R)   (S)

Mirror

Carvone

Diastereomers

Stereoisomers which are not mirror images of each other are called as diastereomers. Diastereomers have similar chemical properties, but have different physical properties. To explain the diasteromers molecule should have minimum two chiral centers. Diastereomers form a pair of enantiomers.

Examples

D-erythrose   L-erythrose

I   II

Enantiomers

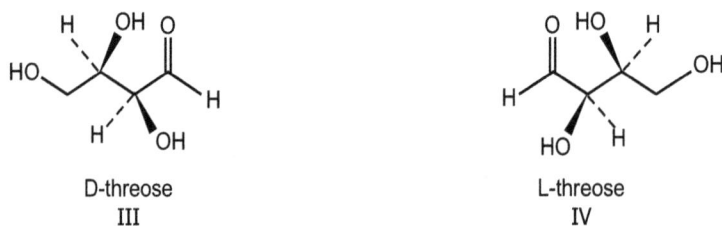

D-threose   L-threose

III   IV

Enantiomers

The possible diastereomers in erythrose. Four isomers will be formed for erythrose sugar. Isomer **I and III** and **II and IV** are the diasteromers of each other. Also, I and IV and II and III isomers are diasteromers of each other.

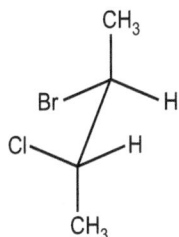

2-bromo-2-chloro butane
I

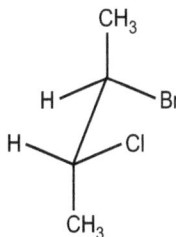

2-bromo-2-chloro butane
II

Enantiomers

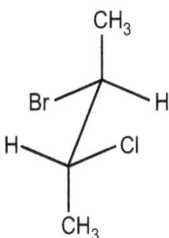

2-bromo-2-chloro butane
III

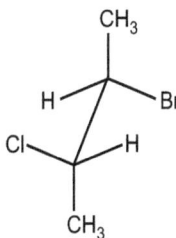

2-bromo-2-chloro butane
IV

Enantiomers

In 2-bromo -2-chlorobutane four isomers are possible **I, II, III and IV and III and II and IV** Isomer I and IV and II and III are diastereomers of each other. Also isomer I and III, II and IV are the diasteromers of each other.

Geometric Isomerism

Geometric isomerism is a form of stereoisomerism. It is also called as **cis-/trans or E/Z** isomerism. It explains the orientation of functional groups within a molecule. The geometric isomerism occurs when the molecule hanged into their spatial positions with respect to one another due to a double bond or a ring structure.

Cis isomer and trans isomer

The name **cis and trans** are derived from Latin, in which **cis** indicate on the same side and **trans** indicate "on the other side or across". As per IUPAC, the term geometric isomerism is outdated term for cis and trans isomers.

Examples

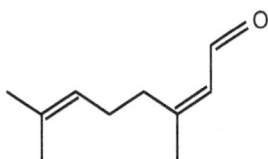

cis-citral

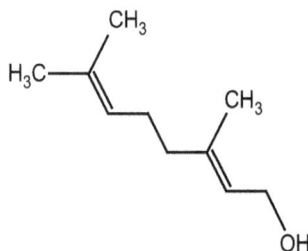

trans-geraniol

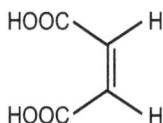

cis-butenedioic acid or maleic acid

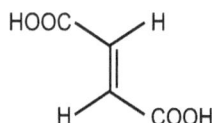

trans-butenedioic acid or furmaric acid

By considering the current IUPAC norms, **E and Z notation** is preferred for explaining the stereochemistry of double bonds instead of **cis/ trans.** Actually, **E and Z** notation is extrapolation of **cis/ trans** nomenclature which are used to refer double bonds having three or four substituent. **E and Z** nomenclature is based on **Cahn-Ingold Priority** rules.

E- notation: The term **E-** is derived from **German** words mean entgegen means opposite. In **E** configuration, the two groups of higher priority are on the opposite sides of the double bonds.

Z- notation : The term **Z-** is derived from **German** word zusammen means together. In **Z** configuration, two groups of higher priority are on the same side of the double bond

Examples

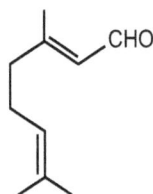

E-citral

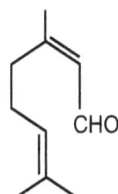

Z-citral

Conformational isomerism: It is also called as conformers. It is a form of steroisomerism in which isomers can be interchanged solely by rotations about single bond.

Resolution of racemic mixture:

It is the process of separation of racemate into its components i.e. separation into dextro and levo forms. Many methods are used for separation of components of racemates. The most commonly exploited methods for separation of racemates are chromatography and use of enzymes.

❖❖❖

BIBLIOGRAPHY

1. Botany, A.C. Datta, 6th Edition 2002, Kolkata, Oxford University Press, New Delhi.

2. Indian Pharmacopocia Vol I - IV, 6th Edition, 1996, Ministry of Health, Govt. of India, New Delhi.

3. Industrial Gums, Polysaccharides and Their Derivatives. Whistler R.L. 1973, Academic press, New York.

4. Pharmacognosy, C.K. Kokate, A.P. Purohit, S.B. Gokhale. 47th Edition, 2012, Nirali Prakashan, Pune 2.

5. Pharmacognosy phytochemistry of medicinal plants, Jean Bruneton, 2nd Edition, 1999. Intercept Ltd. Londers.

6. Pharmacognosy, Trease GE and Evans W.C. 12th Edition 1983, Bailliere Tindall U.K.

7. Pharmacognosy, Tyler E.E. Brady Lyn R and Robbers J.E. Ninth edition, 1988 Burger, Minneaopolis Minnesota. U.S.A.

8. Text book of Pharmacognosy, Wallis T.E., 5th Edition 1967, J & A Churchill Ltd. London (U.K.)

9. Pharmaceutical Biology, Gokahle S.B., Kokate C.K., 7th Edition, 2012, Nirali Prakashan, Pune 2.

10. Medicinal Plants of India Vol. I, 1976, ICMR, New Delhi.

11. Glossary of Indian Medicinal Plants, Chopra R. N., Chopra, J. C. and Nayar S. I., 1956, CSIR, New Delhi.

12. Wealth of India – Raw material series, 1948-1976, Council Scientific and Industrial Research, New Delhi.

13. CRC Hand book of Ayurvedic Medicinal Plants CRC Press Tayler and Francis USA.

14. Indian Materia-Medica Vol. I & II, Third Edition, reprint 2009, Popular Prakashan, Mahalaxmi, Mumbai 26.

15. Biosynthesis of Natural Products: Paulo Manitto, First Edition, 1981, Reprint 2010, Wiley India Pvt. Ltd. 4435-36, Ansari Road Daryaganj, New Delhi 110002.

❖❖❖

THE VITALITY

INDICES

BIOLOGICAL INDEX

❖ ❖ ❖

SYNONYMS INDEX

❖ ❖ ❖

SUBJECT INDEX

❖❖❖

www.ingramcontent.com/pod-product-compliance
Lightning Source LLC
Chambersburg PA
CBHW080557090426
42735CB00016B/3271